HERMITAGE

THE HERMITAGE *AORAKI* MOUNT COOK, NEW ZEALAND

Photography by Mike Langford

FIRST PUBLISHED IN 2002 BY
The Hermitage, *Aoraki* Mount Cook
Private Bag, Mount Cook 7946, NEW ZEALAND
www.hermitage.co.nz
Telephone +64 3 435 1809
Facsimile   +64 3 435 1879

SECOND EDITION PUBLISHED IN 2006

ISBN 0-9582356-1-9

Authors: Franz Blum, Lorenzo Dearie,
Bernd Lippmann & Elmar Strohmeier
Photography by Mike Langford
Photographic Assistant Chris Gleisner
Design and Artwork by Fountaine Design
Some Text by Denis Callesen and Ann Stevenson
Printed in New Zealand by Spectrum Print

The Hermitage Kitchen Team wish to thank
Denis & Christine Callesen for proposing the
creation of this book and special thanks to
John & Trish Davies and family of Queenstown and
Murray & Barbara Valentine of Dunedin for allowing
the 'Hermitage Cuisine' project to proceed.

CONTENTS

MEASUREMENTS

All recipes in this book have been made with New Zealand standard measurements:

t	= teaspoon/s (5ml)
T	= tablespoon/s (15 ml)
C	= cup (250 ml)
°C	= degrees Celsius
L	= litre/s
g	= gram/s
kg	= kilogram/s

CONVERSION TABLE

All measurements rounded to the next full digit

1 g	= 0.0353 oz
28 g	= 1 oz
450 g	= 1 lb
1 kg	= 2 lb 3.3 oz
1 ml	= 0.0352 fl. oz
1 L	= 1 pint 15.2 fl. oz
570 ml	= 1 pint

Conversions given in the recipes may vary from the above as a result of rounding, and approximations may vary depending on the particular ingredient being measured.

TEMPERATURES

°C	°F
120	250
150	300
160	325
180	350
190	375
220	425
250	475

PREFACE FROM THE KITCHEN

The recipes in this book are closely based on the menu of the award-winning Panorama Restaurant of The Hermitage Hotel, and are made for four servings. Most have an haute cuisine origin but have been modified to some degree to make them more straightforward for the home cook to prepare.

Our kitchen is driven by a simple three-part philosophy:
1) The food has a strong international influence. This reflects both our clientele's tastes and the fact that most of our chefs have traveled and worked widely throughout the world.

2) There is a strong focus on quality local produce, in particular from New Zealand's South Island. This helps ensure it is fresh, top quality and distinctive.

3) We encourage our kitchen staff to experiment in a positive environment where any new idea will get a fair trial. It doesn't matter if our most junior chef comes up with a new idea: if it works and our guests like it, we will put it on the menu. Many of our most popular and original dishes have come about this way.

Bon appétit!

THE KITCHEN TEAM

INTRODUCTION

EARLY 1900'S

No menus are to hand from the earliest years but the McDonald family who ran the Hermitage for a while 'made their guests very comfortable and happy, especially enjoying the well cooked meals' and in a letter to his daughter in 1907 McDonald wrote of getting a place of their own: 'The work up here is too much for your mother now as she is not so able as she used to be - we were very busy here this season. The motor cars arriving at all hours and that meant extra dinners to cook, Mollie was kept very busy. I don't know how she manages the cooking for such a number as we've had this season.' (The first cars arrived at Mount Cook in 1906).

ADVERTISEMENT 1907

'The mountain air will give you a splendid appetite. The Hermitage Chef and his assistants are artists in their profession. They have waiting for you, a dinner which not only appeals to the epicure but satisfies the healthy hunger engendered by your long journey. When you step over "The Hermitage" threshold you are 2500 feet above the level of the sea - and you are scores and scores of miles from all your worries and troubles.'

THE 1970'S

Dress codes remained fairly formal, especially for dinner and until the late 1970's spare ties and jackets were kept at the Reception desk for men who hadn't included them in their luggage. Thankfully dress codes today are more relaxed and tidy casual is all that is required. Even the General Manager has dispensed with wearing a tie!

ADVERTISEMENT 1970'S

"The food in the restaurant is superb and the Hermitage offers only the best selections of wine to be found anywhere in NZ."

CONTEMPORARY HERMITAGE

The evening though is still a time for relaxing and enjoying good food and good wines - some things don't change over the years.

SOUPS & ENTRÉES

This spicy, refreshing soup is full of flavour and easily converted into a vegetarian dish by using vegetable stock instead of chicken stock. The hotness is easily adjusted by using more or less chilli. If you make the soup a day in advance the flavour will intensify.

SPICY
TORTILLA SOUP

SOUP

30 ml / 4 T olive oil
1 onion, medium size, diced
½ red capsicum, diced
½ yellow capsicum, diced
½ green capsicum, diced
15 g / 2 t garlic, crushed
800 ml / 3 ¾ C chicken or vegetable stock
10 g / 1 ½ T cumin, ground
salt to taste
pepper to taste
5 tomatoes, deseeded & diced
8 g / 1 t sambal olek
150 ml / ¾ C tomato juice

Heat the oil in a pot, add the cumin and fry over moderate heat for one minute. Add the garlic and fry while stirring continuously until all the flavours are released. This takes about two minutes and the ingredients should not brown. Add the onion, salt and pepper and fry for an additional two minutes. Add the capsicums and fry for a further two to three minutes. Add the sambal olek and two-thirds of the tomatoes and continue frying for a further four minutes. The frying process is very important as it releases all the flavours from the ingredients and gives the soup its distinctive taste. Keep stirring well while frying to ensure that all ingredients are evenly fried and do not burn. Add the stock and tomato juice and simmer for 6-10 minutes. Taste-test and adjust seasoning if necessary.

GARNISH

1 flour tortilla, cut into strips and fried
60 g / ½ C cheddar cheese, grated
12 g / ¼ C fresh coriander, roughly chopped
1 avocado, diced
120 g / ¾ C sweetcorn kernels, cooked

Place the prepared garnish, including the reserved diced tomatoes, in a soup plate or big bowls and pour the hot soup onto it. This soup will last for two to three days in the fridge and can easily be frozen. If you store or freeze the soup, prepare the garnish on the day you will be using it.

SUGGESTED MATCH
Gunn Estate Silistria Syrah

This sweet soup is ideal for cold days. It is really easy to make and the garnish gives a nice touch to the end result. The roasting process is an important step and should be done carefully.

HONEY-GLAZED PUMPKIN AND APPLE
SOUP
WITH WARM DUCK AND ROCKET SALAD

PUMPKIN AND APPLE SOUP

500 g / 3 C pumpkin, peeled
170 ml / ⅔ C honey
6 cloves garlic
150 g / 1 C onions
1 fresh apple
220 ml / 1 C cider
1 L / 4 C water
salt to taste
pepper to taste

Roughly chop pumpkin, garlic, apple and onion and place in a roasting tray. Season and cover with the honey. Roast in a preheated oven at 180°C (360°F) for 20 minutes or until golden brown. Put roasted ingredients into a pot and add the cider. Bring to the boil and simmer over moderate heat until liquid is reduced by a third. Add the water and simmer for a further 25 minutes. Adjust seasoning and blend. Strain through a sieve.

DUCK AND ROCKET SALAD

4 sheets filo pastry
2.5 ml / ½ t pumpkin oil
18 g / ⅛ C pumpkin seeds, roasted
1 duck breast
5 g / 1 t salt
18 g / 1 C rocket leaves, freshly picked

Cut the filo pastry into sixteen 7 x 7 cm (3" x 3") squares. Lay 4 squares on top of each other and press into muffin tins (or on to the backs of espresso-cup-sized bowls) and bake in a preheated oven at a moderate heat until golden brown and crispy. Let cool and reserve for later use. Season the duck with salt and seal it in a very hot pan. Put in a preheated oven at 170°C (340°F) and cook for another six minutes. Rest in a warm place for 10 minutes.

TO SERVE

Mix the rocket leaves, pumpkin seeds, finely sliced duck breast and the pumpkin oil and place in the filo pastry cups. Pour the hot soup into bowls and place cups in the centre. Drizzle some pumpkin oil over the soup and serve immediately.

SUGGESTED MATCH
Wild South Chardonnay

This unusual soup gets most of its flavour from the hay. Using hay for cooking is quite popular in Switzerland, where this dish may have originated. Make sure you use good-quality, clean hay. Grissini are crisp pastry sticks, which are very popular in Italy.

MOUNTAIN
HAY SOUP
WITH CHAMPAGNE VINEGAR AND AIR-DRIED BEEF GRISSINI

MOUNTAIN HAY SOUP

50 g / ¼ C butter
½ onion
25 g / 1 ½ T fresh garlic
3 potatoes, medium size
50 g / ¼ C leek
750 ml / 3 C vegetable stock (see p. 109)
250 ml / 1 C cream
25 g / 1 C firmly packed meadow hay
salt to taste
pepper to taste
10 ml / 2 t champagne vinegar
(or good white wine vinegar)

Peel and roughly chop the onions and potatoes. Peel the garlic and slice thinly. Wash the leek well and cut roughly into pieces. Melt the butter in a pot over a moderate heat and cook the garlic and the onions until light brown. Add all the other vegetables, stir and cook for two to three minutes. Add the vegetable stock and the cream, bring to the boil, reduce the heat and simmer until all vegetables are tender. Blend the soup and season to taste. If the soup is too thick add more vegetable stock to achieve a creamy consistency. Bring back to the boil, add the hay, stir well, take off the heat and leave for ten minutes to infuse. Strain the soup through a fine sieve to remove the hay and add the vinegar. Blend soup until smooth and frothy and serve immediately with the beef wrapped grissini.

GRISSINI

120 g / 1 C flour
20 g / 2 ½ T semolina
1 pinch salt
1 g / ½ t molasses (or treacle, or malt)
80 ml / ⅓ C water
5 g / ¾ t fresh yeast
80 g / 2.8 oz air-dried beef, thinly sliced

Dissolve the yeast in lukewarm water. Add the rest of the ingredients except the beef, and knead to a smooth dough. Cover with a damp cloth and rest the dough in a warm place until it has doubled in volume. Put the dough on a lightly floured surface and knead well. Form a ball, cover with a tea towel and rest for ten minutes. Pat the top to flatten the ball a little. Make two incisions on one side of the ball, as you would cut a tassle but leaving it attached to the dough ball. Grab the 'tassle' by the end and pull while shaking your hand so it forms a finger of dough. Continue pulling until the 'finger' is about 20 cm (8'') long, cut it off and put on a greased oven tray. Repeat until all the dough is used. Bake in a preheated oven at 190°C (380°F) until golden brown and crispy. Leave to cool and wrap the beef tightly around the grissini just before serving.

This easy-to-prepare salad takes almost no time to put together. The lamb fillets can be substituted with any other meat – this salad works particularly well with chicken.

SEARED
LAMB FILLETS
ON HARICOT BEAN, WATERCRESS
AND PUMPKIN SALAD WITH PEA PURÉE

LAMB SALAD

250 g / 8.8 oz lamb fillets
salt to taste
pepper to taste
45 g / ¼ C pumpkin, shaved into strips
100 g / 1 C French beans
2 g / 1 t chives, snipped
50 g / 1 C watercress leaves

Season the lamb fillets and sear them in a very hot pan. Rest them for ten minutes and slice just before serving. Place all vegetables and herbs in a bowl and toss with the dressing. Adjust seasoning if required.

DRESSING

25 ml / 1 ½ t balsamic vinegar
15 ml / 1 T extra virgin olive oil
salt to taste
pepper to taste

Combine all ingredients with a whisk. Season to taste.

PEA PURÉE

75 g / ½ C fresh or frozen green peas
2 g / 1 T fresh mint
50 ml / 3 T chicken stock (see p.108)
salt to taste
pepper to taste

Combine all ingredients in a pot and boil until the peas are tender. Remove from the heat and purée. Pass through a sieve and leave to cool.

TO SERVE

Place the salad in the centre of the plates and top with the sliced lamb fillets. Drizzle the pea purée around the salad. Serve immediately.

SUGGESTED MATCH
Sacred Hill Wine Thief Merlot

This lovely light parfait is a nice start to a menu. It can also be made with other liver, e.g. chicken liver, and the emu meat can be substituted by any other red game meat. If you cannot obtain truffles use mushrooms soaked in water.

DUCK LIVER AND EMU
PARFAIT
ON FRESH GREENS
WITH ITALIAN VINAIGRETTE AND FLAT CRISP BREAD

DUCK LIVER PARFAIT

50 g / ⅓ C onions, finely diced
50 ml / ¼ C madeira or sherry
100 g / ⅓ C jus (see p. 108)
50 g / ¼ C truffle juice
(or soaking liquid from the dried mushrooms)
100 g / ⅓ C duck livers
30 g / 2 T sour cream
20 g / 1 ½ T black truffles, finely diced
250 ml / 1 C cream, whipped
150 g / 5.3 oz emu meat
40 g / 2 ¼ T butter, cold
salt to taste
pepper to taste

Sauté the onions and emu lightly for five minutes. Add the madeira the jus and truffle juice and reduce on moderate heat to a syrupy consistency. Take off the heat and leave to cool. Fry the livers in a pan until evenly seared and allow to cool. Combine the liver, emu meat, sour cream and seasoning and purée in a food processor until very smooth. Add the butter and purée until combined. Put the mixture in a bowl, add the truffle and carefully fold the cream through the mixture. Put the parfait in a bowl and leave to set in the fridge (at least two hours).

VINAIGRETTE

100 ml / ⅓ C olive oil
5 g / ½ t salt
1 g / ¼ t pepper
50 ml / 3 T red wine vinegar
10 ml / 2 t balsamic vinegar
5 g / ½ t English mustard
20 ml / 1 T water

Combine all ingredients and whisk.

FLAT CRISP BREAD

150 g / 1 ¼ C plain white flour
65 ml / ¼ C warm water
10 g / ½ T butter, soft but not melted

Combine the flour and water. Add the butter and knead in a food processor on low speed for five minutes. Form the dough into a ball, cover with a damp cloth and rest for one hour. Work the dough for another two to three minutes and divide into golfball-sized pieces. Roll the pieces as thinly as you can and cook in a hot non-stick pan (no oil) until dry and crispy. Cut into triangles while the bread is still hot.

HERB SALAD

Equal quantities of rocket, baby spinach, watercress & beetroot leaves

TO SERVE

Arrange the green leaves in the middle of the plate and drizzle with the vinaigrette. Form two egg-shaped portions of the parfait with a hot spoon (like making an ice-cream ball) and place on the leaves. Serve with the bread.

The combination of smoked salmon and horseradish works really well and is used in a lot of classical recipes. This dish is simple to prepare and looks appealing on the plate. We smoke our own salmon, and an easy way of doing this is described on p. 97.

SMOKED SALMON
MILLE-FEUILLE
ON ROCKET LEAVES WITH LYCHEE AND WALNUT DRESSING

CRÊPES

60 g / ½ C flour
1 egg
150 ml / ½ C milk
salt to taste
5 g / 1 t chives
20 g / 1 T butter

Combine all ingredients except the chives in a blender and run at medium speed for five minutes. Add the finely sliced chives and adjust seasoning if necessary. Cook in a small pan like pancakes, as thin as you possibly can. Allow crêpes to cool. You will need 16 crêpes.

SMOKED SALMON MILLE-FEUILLE

10 g / 1 T chives
20 g / 1 ½ T fresh horseradish, finely grated
150 ml / ½ C cream, whipped
4 crêpes
200 g / 7 oz smoked salmon

Whip the cream and add the grated horseradish. Put four crêpes on a tray and spread thinly with the horseradish cream. Top with the thinly sliced smoked salmon and spread another thin layer of the horseradish cream on top. Repeat the layering until you have four layers of crêpes, finishing the mille-feuilles with a layer of horseradish cream, and freeze for one hour. To achieve nice edges cut the half-frozen mille-feuilles with a 7cm (3") pastry cutter. Allow the pieces to finish defrosting. Sprinkle the top of each mille-feuille with the finely sliced chives before serving.

LYCHEE AND WALNUT DRESSING

30 ml / 2 T walnut oil
20 ml / 1 ½ T white wine vinegar
20 g / 1 ½ T tinned lychees, finely diced
salt and pepper to taste
40 g / 3 ¾ T lychee juice
5 g / 1 T roasted walnuts, roughly chopped
10 g / 1 T walnuts, whole roasted, for garnish
4 rocket leaves

Combine all ingredients with a whisk and adjust seasoning if needed.

TO SERVE

Place rocket leaves in the centre of the plate and drizzle with the lychee and walnut dressing. Place the smoked salmon mille-feuille on the rocket leaves and sprinkle with roasted walnuts. Garnish with two pieces of chives and a roasted walnut.

SUGGESTED MATCH
Sacred Hill Sauvage Sauvignon Blanc

In this dish the tuna is just quickly seared: do not cook it any further as it will change the lovely balance of flavours in the dish and make the tuna too dry. All the ingredients can be obtained in the herb or Asian section of your supermarket.

SESAME-COATED
TUNA MEDALLIONS
ON PROVENÇALE VEGETABLE SALSA WITH BOUILLABAISSE SAUCE

SESAME-COATED TUNA

320 g / 11 oz fresh tuna loin
15 g / 2 T tahini (sesame paste)
25 g / 4 T black sesame seeds (keep some for garnish)
20 g / 3 T white sesame seeds
20 ml / 1 ¼ T sesame oil
salt to taste
pepper to taste

Coat the loins thinly with tahini and season with salt and pepper. Mix the sesame seeds and place them on a plate. Roll the tuna through the seeds until evenly coated. Heat a frying pan and add the sesame oil. Sear the tuna on all sides until the white sesame seeds are golden brown. Remove from the pan and leave to cool. Wrap in cling film and place in fridge for later use.

BOUILLABAISSE SAUCE

30 ml / 2 T olive oil
30 g / ⅓ C leek (white flesh only)
40 g / ½ C fennel bulb
1 clove garlic, crushed
1 pinch saffron
1 g / 1 t fresh oregano
1 g / 1 t fresh sweet fennel
300 ml / 1 C fish stock (see p. 109)
4 plum tomatoes
50 ml / 3 ¼ T dry vermouth
4 sprigs fresh basil

Dice all vegetables roughly and keep separate. Sauté all vegetables except the tomatoes in the olive oil over moderate heat until soft - ensure vegetables do not colour. Add the tomatoes and cook for a further two minutes. Add the vermouth and reduce until no liquid is left. Add the fish stock and saffron and reduce by half. Season and remove from the heat. Add the herbs and purée in a blender until very smooth. Strain through a fine sieve, adjust seasoning if necessary and leave to cool.

VEGETABLE SALSA

1 recipe vegetable salsa (see p. 112)

TO SERVE

Slice the tuna in 12 equal slices and place 3 pieces per portion off-centre on the plate. Put the vegetable salsa into a 3.5cm (1.5") pastry cutter and place behind the tuna. Remove the cutter, drizzle the sauce around the plate and sprinkle a few black sesame seeds over the plate. Top the vegetable salsa with cherry tomatoes and a sprig of oregano.

GARNISH

4 half red cherry tomatoes
4 half yellow cherry tomatoes
4 sprigs oregano
4 sprigs chervil

SUGGESTED MATCH
Sacred Hill Barrel Fermented Chardonnay

Prepare the duck legs between 6 and 12 hours ahead to allow the flavours to penetrate the meat. If you cannot obtain duck fat it can be substituted with the same quantity of olive oil. The spices for the lime pickle should preferably be freshly ground.

FIVE-SPICE ROASTED
DUCK LEG
ON CRISP FENNEL WITH LIME PICKLE

FIVE-SPICE DUCK LEG

4 duck legs
700 g / 3 ½ C duck fat, rendered
10 g / 2 T five-spice powder
100 g / ⅓ C rock salt
100 g / ½ C brown sugar crystals

Mix the rock salt, sugar and five-spice powder in a shallow tray and roll the duck legs through it, covering evenly. Leave legs in the tray, cover with cling film and leave in the fridge to infuse flavours (not longer than 12 hours). Wash the duck legs under running water, pat dry and place in a roasting tray. Top with the melted duck fat so that the legs are about 90 percent covered, and bake at 110°C (230°F) for approx. two and a half hours or until very tender. Remove from the fat and set aside.

FENNEL SALAD

1 fennel bulb
1 sprig sweet fennel, finely chopped
5 g / ½ t Dijon mustard
4 g / ½ t fresh ginger, grated
60 g / ⅓ C red onions, sliced
15 ml / 1 T cider vinegar
30 ml / 2 T olive oil
salt and pepper to taste

Slice the fennel bulb and red onions very finely and combine with other ingredients. Reserve.

SWEET LIME PICKLE

8 limes, segmented (see p. 116)
4 g / 1 T cardamom pods
3 g / 2 ½ t coriander seeds
3 g / 2 ½ t black mustard seeds
1 fresh red chilli, small
3 curry leaves
60 g / ½ C onions, sliced
100 g / ½ C sugar
10 ml / 2 t olive oil

Grind the spices and cook them in preheated oil with the onions and finely chopped chilli for three to four minutes. Add the lime segments and cook for another three minutes. Add the sugar and boil until the sugar turns golden brown. Remove from the heat. Rest for at least six hours or bottle in sterilized jars. Improves with keeping.

TO SERVE

Place some fennel salad in the centre of the plate and put one duck leg on top. Spoon lime pickle onto it, garnish with the thinly sliced lime and a sprig of sweet fennel and serve.

SUGGESTED MATCH
Sacred Hill Marlborough Pinot Noir

Following are three ways of preparing this delicious shellfish.

Each way gives you a different end result while retaining the delicate

flavour of the scallops. If you develop a favorite out of the three it

can be easily used by itself as an appetizer or main course.

TRIO OF
SCALLOPS
FROM NEW ZEALAND

SCALLOP TARTARE

12 scallops
3 drops Worcestershire sauce
3 drops Tabasco sauce
½ bunch fresh chives, chopped
½ tomato, peeled and fine diced
salt to taste
8 pieces of chives for garnish

Remove the roe (the orange part) from the scallops. (Reserve roe if also making the poached scallops recipe.) Chop the scallops roughly and add all other ingredients. Taste and adjust seasoning if necessary. Store in the fridge until needed.

RASPBERRY REDUCTION

100 g / ½ C raspberry vinegar
50 g / ½ C fresh raspberries
50 g / ¼ C sugar

Combine all ingredients, bring to the boil and reduce to a syrupy consistency. Leave in a warm place for later use.

GRILLED SCALLOPS WITH GINGER AND LIME DRESSING

15ml / 1 T olive oil, for frying
12 scallops
20 ml / 1 ¼ T lime juice
100 ml / ⅓ C sunflower oil
4 cloves garlic
salt to taste
pepper to taste
20 g / 1 ¼ T ginger
20 g / 2 T rice vinegar
20 g / 2 T mirin

First make the dressing. Combine all ingredients apart from the scallops and whisk (do not use a blender) in a bowl. Preheat a pan with a little olive oil and sear the scallops for approx. two minutes. The scallops should be just cooked (warm in the middle). Take the scallops out and deglaze the pan with the ginger and lime dressing.

POACHED SCALLOPS WITH WHITE WINE ROE SAUCE

8 scallops
50 g / ¼ C white wine
1 pinch salt
100 ml / ⅓ C cream
4 sprigs fresh chervil for garnish

Cut the scallops horizontally in half. Arrange on a tray, season and sprinkle with the white wine. Place under a grill until cooked. Take the scallops off the tray and pour the liquid into a pot. Reduce by a third and add the cream. Boil for another two minutes and remove from the heat. Add the roe which you have left from the tartare recipe. Blend to a smooth, frothy sauce.

POTATO AND PARMESAN CHEESE CRACKER

100 g / ½ C potato, cooked and mashed
30 g / 2 ¼ T parmesan cheese, grated
1 egg yolk
3 g / 2 T fresh chervil, chopped

Combine potato with parmesan cheese, egg yolks and chopped chervil and mix well. Spread thinly as possible into little square shapes on a greased baking tray (see the tuille recipe in the Mount Cook Soufflé recipe p.72) and bake in a preheated oven at 180°C (360°F) until golden brown. While the crackers are still hot, trim the edges with a sharp knife into uniform squares. Let cool and reserve for later use.

SUGGESTED MATCH
Sacred Hill Marlborough Riesling

continued...

TO SERVE

(described for plating on a plate - varies from photo)
Put a small round pastry cutter on a plate and fill with a quarter of the tartare. Remove the cutter and drizzle the raspberry reduction in dots around the tartare. Arrange the grilled scallops and top with the ginger and lime dressing.
Put two poached scallop halves on the plate and top with a cracker, top with another half and top with another cracker. Place the remaining scallop half on top and drizzle some of the white wine sauce around the poached scallops.
Garnish the poached scallops with a sprig of chervil and arrange two pieces of chives over the tartar. Place a scallop shell on the plate and sprinkle with some cracked pepper. Serve immediately.

This New Zealand-farmed shellfish is exported all over the world. It is bigger and tastier than its black-shelled cousins, and available fresh or frozen. Fresh ones are best but if you are not able to obtain them you can use frozen mussels.

GREENSHELL™ MUSSELS
WITH PINOT GRIS SABAYON

GREENSHELL™ MUSSELS

28 fresh mussels
1 carrot
1 onion
2 stems celery
500 ml / 2 C pinot gris wine
250 ml / 1 C water

Brush the mussels under cold water and clean them thoroughly. Discard any that are broken. Grab the 'beard' of each and pull downwards to remove it. Rinse the mussels and put them in a colander to drain. Peel the onion and the carrot and wash the celery. Dice the vegetables finely. Bring water, wine and vegetables to the boil and simmer for 10 minutes. Add the mussels, cover and simmer for four to five minutes. Remove the mussels from the cooking liquid and discard any unopened mussels. Leave any vegetables that might be stuck in the shells. Cover the mussels with a wet cloth. Strain the cooking liquid into another pot, reserving the vegetables for the garnish. Put the liquid on low heat for reheating the mussels after you have done the sabayon.

PINOT GRIS SABAYON

75 ml / ¼ C cooking liquid from the mussels
75 ml / ¼ C pinot gris
2 egg yolks
salt to taste
pepper to taste

Put all ingredients into a heatproof glass or metal bowl. Beat over a hot water bath until you have a very airy and fluffy foam.

GARNISH

4 sprigs sweet fennel or dill
red capsicum strips

TO SERVE

Arrange the mussels in a serving dish and top with the sabayon. Sprinkle with the vegetables and garnish with a sprig of sweet fennel or dill and some red capsicum strips.

SUGGESTED MATCH
Sacred Hill White Cabernet

Sweetbreads are a delicacy used extensively in classical French cuisine. Crépine is an other word for pig's caul, which is a 'fat net'. Always soak crépine for at least two hours in cold water before using it.

LAMB SWEETBREADS
CRÉPINETTE
BRAISED IN WHITE PORT SAUCE WITH
PLUM TOMATO COMPOTE

CRÉPINETTE

320 g / 11oz sweetbreads
240 g / 1 C chicken breasts
150 ml / 1 C cream
50 g / ¼ C crépine
salt to taste
pepper to taste
30 ml / 2 T oil

Bring a pot of salted water to the boil and blanch the sweetbreads for one minute. Remove and place straight into ice water. Leave until cold, peel all the membrane off the sweetbreads and pull them into hazelnut-sized pieces. Season very well with salt and pepper and fry sweetbreads in very hot oil until golden brown on all sides. Remove from the pan and allow to cool. Remove all skin and fat from the chicken breasts and blend with salt and pepper in a food processor until very smooth. Put into a cooled bowl and slowly fold the liquid cream under the chicken. Stir gently with a wooden spoon until the mixture is light and smooth. Rest in the fridge for 30 minutes. Combine the chicken mixture with the cold sweetbreads. Place the soaked crépine onto the work surface and cut into four 15cm (6") squares. Divide the mixture into four balls. Place a ball in the centre of each crépine and fold like an envelope to cover the entire filling. Form into a ball and wrap tightly with cling film. Rest for a further 30 minutes. Heat a little oil in a pan, remove the cling film and brown the crépinettes evenly on all sides. Put into a preheated oven and roast for 12 minutes at 180°C (360°F), turning the crépinettes every three minutes to ensure even cooking.

WHITE PORT BROTH

50 ml / 3 T white port
100 ml / ⅓ C chicken stock (see p.108)
2 shallots
30 g / 2 T fava beans
30 g / 1 ½ T butter
salt to taste
pepper to taste

Remove the fava beans from pods. Slice the shallots finely and cook them with the beans in butter until shallots are soft. Season with salt and pepper and add the white port and chicken stock. Simmer for one minute and reserve for later use.

TOMATO COMPOTE

10 g / 1 T garlic, sliced lengthwise
6 plum tomatoes, peeled, quartered and deseeded
15 ml / 1 T olive oil
80 ml / ⅓ C white wine
salt to taste
pepper to taste

Heat the olive oil over moderate heat and fry the garlic until golden brown. Add the tomatoes and cook for 30 seconds. Add the white wine and simmer over low heat until liquid is reduced by half. Season to taste.

TO SERVE
Bring the white port and fava bean broth to the boil and remove from the heat. Place the tomato compote in the centre of the plate and spoon the broth evenly around the outside of the compote. Cut the sweetbreads in half and place on top of the tomato compote. Serve immediately.

A granité is a nice variation of a sorbet and is much easier to prepare without an ice-cream machine. The lemon juice offsets the sweetness of the fruit; the sweeter the kiwifruits are the more lemon juice you will need.

YELLOW AND GREEN
KIWIFRUIT
AND NOBLE RIESLING GRANITÉ

YELLOW KIWIFRUIT GRANITÉ

50 g / ¼ C yellow kiwifruit
15 ml / 1 T sugar syrup (see below)
3 ml / ¾ T lemon juice

Peel the kiwifruits and squash them through a sieve. (Do not use a blender because it may damage the seeds and make the pulp bitter.) Add the sugar syrup and the lemon juice and combine well. Pour the mixture on a small flat tray and freeze.

GREEN KIWIFRUIT GRANITÉ

50 g / ¼ C green kiwifruit
15 ml / 1 T sugar syrup
3 ml / ¾ T lemon juice

As above.

NOBLE RIESLING GRANITÉ

100 ml / ⅓ C noble riesling
20 g / 4 t sugar
1 mint leaf

Chop the mint finely and combine all ingredients. Pour the mixture on a flat tray and freeze.

SUGAR SYRUP

Bring equal amounts by weight of sugar and water to the boil. Cool.

TO SERVE

Take the green kiwifruit granité out of the freezer and crush it finely. Repeat with the other two granites and layer them into cooled glasses. Garnish with a mint tip and serve immediately. Do not use silver spoons, as this will taint the granité.

MAIN COURSES

This Asian-influenced dish has a delightful combination of flavours. It is really easy and quick to make and a perfect main course. We use fresh baby salmon from the Mount Cook Salmon Farm. The baby salmon can be substituted with fresh trout or any pan-sized freshwater fish.

MOUNT COOK
BABY SALMON
ON ASIAN VEGETABLE AND KUMARA STIR-FRY
WITH A LIGHT GARLIC AND SOYA-MIRIN GLAZE

BABY SALMON

4 baby salmon
10 g / 1 ½ T paprika
100 g / 1 C flour
100 g / 1 C cornflour
salt and pepper to taste
500 ml / 2 C peanut oil
coriander leaves, roughly chopped, for garnish

Clean the inside of the fish thoroughly. Make fine incisions just through the skin on both sides of the fish, taking care not to cut too deep into the flesh. Just before you are ready to serve, season the salmon and combine the flour, cornflour and paprika. Roll the salmon through this mixture and fry in very hot oil until golden brown and crispy. Place salmon on a paper towel to absorb excess fat.

VEGETABLE STIR-FRY

20 ml / 1 ¼ T sesame oil
70 g / 1 C mung beans
60 g / 2.2 oz bok choi (Chinese cabbage)
150 g / 1 ½ C kumara (sweet potato)
1 spring onion
120 g / 4.2 oz carrots
150 g / 5.2 oz courgettes
100 g / 3.5 oz bamboo shoots
1 clove garlic

Slice all vegetables into attractive shapes. Heat the sesame oil in a wok or frying pan and stir-fry all ingredients, maintaining a slight crunchiness. Do not season, as the sauce will provide all the flavours.

SOYA AND MIRIN SAUCE

60 ml / ¼ C soya sauce
120 ml / ½ C mirin
20 g / 1 ½ T ginger, fresh, finely diced
2 cloves garlic
10 g / 1 T butter

Heat the butter, add the garlic and ginger and toss quickly to release the flavours. Add the mirin and bring to the boil. Add the soya sauce and remove from the heat. Keep in a warm place until needed.

TO SERVE

Arrange the vegetables on a plate and place the salmon on top. Sprinkle with the chopped coriander and pour the sauce over the salmon. Garnish with coriander and serve immediately.

SUGGESTED MATCH

Sacred Hill Riflemans Chardonnay

Although other white fish can be substituted, most people who have tried blue cod would agree it is one of New Zealand's finest fish. Chorizo sausage is usually bought, but the home-made variety is hard to beat so the recipe is given here.

PAN-FRIED
BLUE COD
IN TARRAGON BROTH WITH FRESH
SPINACH LEAVES AND CHORIZO SAUSAGES

BLUE COD

800 g / 28 oz blue cod fillets
50 ml / 3 ¼ T oil
salt to taste
pepper to taste

Cut the fillets into equal-sized portions and season. Just before serving, pan-fry until golden brown and cooked.

TARRAGON BROTH

6 shallots, sliced
140 g / 1 C black-eyed beans
150 ml / ½ C chicken stock (see p. 108)
4 g / 1 t fresh tarragon
50 g / 3 T butter
salt to taste
pepper to taste
50 g / 3 T acid-free tomatoes, deseeded and diced

Soak beans overnight in cold water, then boil in salted water for 25 minutes or until tender. Sautée the shallots in half of the butter without colouring. Add the cooked beans and stock and reduce by a third. Add the tarragon, simmer for two more minutes and remove from the heat. Slowly add the rest of the butter while stirring continuously. Lastly add the tomatoes and season to taste.

SPINACH

160 g / 3 C baby spinach leaves
salt to taste
pepper to taste

Wash the spinach thoroughly and remove all big stalks. Just before serving, steam for 10 seconds until just wilted and season lightly.

CHORIZO SAUSAGES

450 g / 1lb pork chuck
150 g / 1 C pork fat
1 g / ¼ t cumin, ground
1 g / ¼ t cayenne pepper
1 g / ¼ t oregano
4 cloves garlic, crushed
2 red chilli, finely chopped
15 ml / 1 T red wine vinegar
1 g / ¼ t mint leaves
40 cm / 16" sausage skins, 15mm (5/8 in) diameter

Combine all ingredients, mince and rest for six hours. Soak the sausage skins until soft and fill them with the meat mixture. Roast in a preheated oven at 180°C (360°F) for 10 minutes.

TO SERVE

Cut the chorizos and place into the hot broth. Place the spinach in the centre of a soup plate and arrange the fish on top. Pour the hot broth over the fish and serve immediately.

This dish is tasty and easy to make with any type of lobster or crayfish. The New Zealand rock lobster is closely related to the langouste of French cuisine and the South African crawfish. If you cannot obtain whitebait the timbale can be made without it.

NEW ZEALAND
ROCK LOBSTER
ON TOMATO-MARJORAM COMPOTE
WITH WILD RICE AND WHITEBAIT TIMBALE AND GRILLED FENNEL

ROCK LOBSTER

4 rock lobsters
40 ml / 2 ½ T olive oil
5 drops lemon juice
2 drops Tabasco sauce
salt to taste
pepper to taste
mustard cress to garnish

Put the fresh rock lobsters head-first into boiling water for 30 seconds. Remove and place immediately into ice water. Cut the lobster lengthwise in half, remove the internal organs (discard the stomach and feathery gills) and blend the lobster with oil, lemon juice, Tabasco sauce and the seasoning. Brush the lobster with the oil mixture and grill in oven until cooked (about ten minutes).

TOMATO AND MARJORAM COMPOTE

5 tomatoes
5 g / ¼ C fresh marjoram, chopped
60 g / ⅓ C shallots
10 g / 2 t garlic
20 ml / 1 ¼ T extra virgin olive oil
20 ml / 1 T balsamic vinegar
salt to taste
pepper to taste

Peel, de-seed and dice the tomatoes. Dice the garlic and shallots finely and combine all ingredients. Leave to marinate for two hours.

WILD RICE AND WHITEBAIT TIMBALE

65 g / ⅓ C wild rice
120 g / ¾ C whitebait
2 eggs
salt to taste
pepper to taste
20 g / 1 ¼ T butter, softened
2 g / 1 T fresh coriander

Cook the wild rice until soft, strain and cool. Separate the eggs and whisk the egg whites until stiff. Beat the soft butter and egg yolks until creamy and combine with the rice, whitebait and coriander. Gently fold the stiff egg whites through the rice mixture. Fill buttered and floured timbales and bake in a preheated oven at 180°C (360°F) for nine minutes. Rest for five minutes before unmoulding the timbales.

GRILLED FENNEL

2 fennel bulbs
10 ml / 2 t olive oil
salt to taste
pepper to taste
30 ml / 2 T lemon juice
1 sprig sweet fennel

Thinly slice the fennel bulbs lengthwise and marinate with other ingredients for an hour. Remove from the marinade and grill until golden.

TO SERVE

Arrange the grilled fennel in the centre of a plate and place the timbale on top. Place the lobster next to it and drizzle the cold tomato compote around the plate. Garnish the rock lobster with mustard cress.
Serve immediately .

The crispness of the scampi is achieved by coating them in crushed cornflakes, which also enhances their natural sweetness. The jus used for the sauce can either be bought from a delicatessen or can be home-made if you have plenty of time.

CRISPY-FRIED
SCAMPI

WITH THAI-STYLE PINEAPPLE RICE, CURRIED OKRA AND SAUCE AMÉRICAINE

CRISPY SCAMPI

20 scampi
250 ml / 1 C vegetable oil
50 g / ½ C flour
2 eggs, beaten
100 g / 2 C cornflakes, crushed
salt to taste

Remove the head from each scampi by twisting and pulling apart. Reserve the heads for later use in the sauce. Peel the tails (again reserving the shell) but leave the very last segment with the tail fins on. Wash the tails and put in the fridge for later use.

CURRIED OKRA

5 g / 1 t green curry paste
50 g / ⅓ C onions, diced
50 g / ⅓ C tomatoes, chopped
75 ml / ¼ C tomato juice
salt to taste
24 okra
30 ml / 2 T oil

Start by preparing the curry sauce. Fry the diced onions in the oil over low heat until light brown. Add the curry paste, tomatoes and tomato juice and boil for five minutes. Just before serving fry the okra, add just enough curry sauce to coat them and cook for another two minutes. Season to taste.

SAUCE AMÉRICAINE

Reserved scampi heads & shells, chopped
40 ml / 2 ½ T oil
35 g / ¼ C carrot
35 g / ¼ C celery
40 g / ⅓ C onion
50 ml / 4 T brandy
50 ml / 3 T white wine
400 ml / 1 ½ C jus (see p. 108)
250 ml / 1 C fish stock (see p. 109)
juice of 1 lime

Wash the vegetables and chop finely. Put the oil in a pot and stir-fry the vegetables on low heat until soft. Meanwhile heat a pan, add the oil and fry the scampi parts over a high heat for two minutes. Do not stir too often or remove the pan from the heat, as this will draw water out of the scampi heads and boil them instead of frying them, which greatly changes the flavour. Add the brandy and wine, boil to loosen all residues from the pan and add to the vegetables. Add the jus and fish stock, bring to the boil and simmer for one and a half hours. Skim frequently throughout the whole cooking time. Strain through a fine sieve and reduce on low heat until a syrupy consistency is achieved. Just before serving add the lime juice.

continued...

THAI-STYLE PINEAPPLE RICE

2 baby pineapples
1 fresh red chilli, finely chopped
10 g / ¼ C spring onion, finely sliced
20 g / ¼ C fine dessicated coconut
1 clove garlic, crushed
25 g / 1 T butter
200 g / 1 ½ C basmati rice, cooked
3 shallots, finely diced

Cut the baby pineapples in half lengthwise and carefully remove the flesh without breaking the skin. Keep the skins for arranging on the plates. Finely dice the pineapple flesh. Heat the butter in a frying pan and add the coconut, shallots, chilli, garlic, spring onion and pineapple and toss quickly without colouring. Add the rice and mix thoroughly. Add a dash of water and quickly cover with a lid to reheat the rice thoroughly. Keep in a warm place for serving.

TO SERVE

Roll the scampi tails in flour then dip in the egg, then in the crushed corn-flakes and fry in the hot oil until crisp and golden brown. Remove and put on a paper towel to drain. Fill the pineapple skins with the rice and arrange all ingredients on a plate.

The natural sweetness and different textures of the ingredients give this dish its unique quality. The lamb rack takes a bit of preparation and great care has to be taken when cooking it. Once you cut the finished roulade you will see the nice colour contrast.

LAMB RACK
ROULADE

**FILLED WITH MACADAMIA NUTS AND FRESH MANGO ON
LAVENDER JUS WITH CAPSICUM RAGOUT AND KUMARA SOUFFLE**

LAMB RACK ROULADE

4 (approx. 250gm (9oz) each) frenched lamb racks
salt to taste
pepper to taste
40 ml / 2 ½ T maple syrup
100 g / 1 C macadamia nuts, roughly chopped
100 g / ¾ C mango, diced
butchers string
oil to cook

Trim all sinews and fat off the meat. With a sharp knife scrape all skin and meat remains off the bones. This is a time-consuming job but pays off when presenting the roulade on the plate. Reserve all the offcuts and scrapings. Now take a sharp knife and run down the bones to loosen the meat (see photos below) — take great care not to cut the meat completely off the bone! Turn your knife horizontal and cut while you pull the meat gently away from the bone. The end result should look like a schnitzel attached to bones. Repeat with the other racks. Lay the meat out and cover with cling film. Flatten the meat with a heavy knife or meat hammer, taking care not to make holes through the meat.

Season the meat with salt and pepper and brush with maple syrup. Cover the meat evenly with the nuts and the mangoes. Now roll the meat tightly towards the bones. The lamb rack roulade should end up almost looking like the rack did before you started. Tie the meat to the bones at both ends and in the middle to ensure the roulade does not open while cooking, and cover the exposed bones with foil. Sear the racks in a hot pan and roast at 190°C (380°F) in the oven to your liking (we recommend medium rare). Rest in a warm place for 10 minutes and remove the foil.

LAVENDER JUS

Offcuts & scrapings from lamb racks (see previous page)
250 ml / 1 C beef stock (see p. 108)
150 ml / ½ C red wine
salt to taste
pepper to taste
8 sprigs lavender for garnish

Fry the offcuts until dark brown. Add the red wine, reduce by half and add the stock. Simmer for 30 minutes and strain. Put back on the heat and reduce to a syrupy consistency. Take off the heat and add the lavender. Leave to infuse for 10 minutes. Adjust seasoning, strain again and reserve for later.

CAPSICUM RAGOUT

1 red capsicum
1 yellow capsicum
1 green capsicum
40 g / ¼ C shallots, diced
2 tomatoes, de-seeded and diced
salt to taste
pepper to taste
50 ml / 3 T olive oil
100 ml / 6 T tomato juice
40 g / ¼ C tomato paste

De-seed the capsicums and cut them into little diamonds. Heat the olive oil in a pan and cook the capsicums and shallots for five minutes. Stir in the tomatoes and tomato paste and cook for another two to three minutes. Add the tomato juice, simmer for five minutes and adjust seasoning.

SUGGESTED MATCH
Sacred Hill BP Merlot Cabernet

continued...

KUMARA SOUFFLÉ

320 g / 11 oz kumara (sweet potato)
2 egg yolks
1 egg white
salt to taste
pepper to taste
1 pinch nutmeg

Peel the kumara, cut roughly and boil in salted water until soft. Strain and add the egg yolks and seasoning and mash. Whisk the egg white until stiff and fold gently through the kumara mixture. Fill into greased and floured forms and bake in a preheated oven at 180°C (360°F) for 8-10 minutes.

TO SERVE

Cut a one-bone cutlet off the lamb rack. Place the lamb rack onto the plate and spoon the capsicum ragout in front of it. Put the single cutlet onto the capsicum ragout, leaning it against the rack. Pour some sauce onto the plate and put the kumara soufflé straight out of the oven onto the plate. Garnish with two lavender flowers and serve.

The glaze for this dish is more or less a barbecue sauce. If you want to save some time buy a good-quality barbecue sauce; however, time spent making your own sauce is never wasted.

SWEET SMOKED TOMATO-GLAZED
GAME HEN
WITH ONION SWEETBREADS PUDDING,
WILTED GREENS AND CORN RELISH

GAME HEN

4 rock Cornish game hens, or poussins

1 recipe sweet smoked tomato glaze
(see p. 113)

Clean the birds thoroughly, pat dry and marinate in the tomato glaze for one to two hours. Put them in a preheated roasting tray and roast in a fan oven at 180°C (360°F) for 25 minutes or until cooked. During the roasting process brush several times with the marinade.

SWEETBREADS PUDDING

240 g / 1 C sweetbreads, poached and peeled
(see page 32)
50 g / ½ C white bread, 1-cm dice
100 g / 1 C red onions, thinly sliced
5 g / 1 t garlic, finely sliced
2 g / ¼ t butter
25 ml / 1 ½ T cream
3 g / 1 t paprika
1 g / ¼ t fresh thyme
8 g / 2 t Worcestershire sauce
25 g / 2 T parmesan cheese
2 eggs
20 ml / 1 ¼ T olive oil
25 g / ¼ C flour
salt to taste
pepper to taste

Fry the sweetbreads in oil until golden brown. Season with salt and pepper, add the garlic and the onions and cook until soft. Remove from the heat and put into a bowl. Combine with the rest of the ingredients and correct seasoning if necessary. Butter four moulds 6 cm (2.5") wide and 4 cm (1.5") high and fill them, ensuring the sweetbreads are evenly distributed. Bake in a preheated oven at 150°C (300°F) for 14 minutes. Rest for several minutes in a warm place before using.

WILTED GREENS

90 g / 2 C spinach
75 g / 1 ½ C rocket
60 g / 1 C watercress
salt to taste
pepper to taste
50 ml / 3 T extra virgin olive oil
40 ml / 2 ½ T white wine vinegar

Pick the leaves of the spinach, rocket and watercress off the stems and discard the stems. Combine vinegar, oil, salt and pepper to make a vinaigrette. Reserve for later use.

CORN RELISH

1 recipe corn relish (see p. 113)

TO SERVE

Bring the vinaigrette to the boil and combine with the prepared greens. Arrange the wilted greens in the middle of the plate and place the game hen on top of it. Spoon some corn relish around the plate and drizzle some tomato glaze onto the plate. Serve immediately.

The fillet or tenderloin is the best and most tender cut of beef. The marinade we use is a mixture of brown sugar, rock salt and cracked pepper which brings out the excellent flavour. The flavours of the sauce and side dishes are in perfect harmony.

MARINATED
BEEF FILLET
ON SPINACH CREAM SAUCE
WITH OLIVE POTATOES AND TOMATO COMPOTE

BEEF FILLET

800 g / 28 oz beef fillet
15 g / 2 T cracked black pepper
60 g / ⅓ C brown sugar crystals
30 g / 2 T rock salt
20 ml / 1 ¼ T oil to cook

Trim all sinew and fat off the beef fillet. Mix the cracked pepper, rock salt and brown sugar. Cut a piece of cling film slightly longer than the fillet and place on a bench. Spread the salt mixture evenly over the cling film and roll the beef fillet in it, covering evenly. Wrap tightly, ensuring you get a nice round shape. Leave to marinate for two to three hours in the fridge. Unwrap the fillet and cut into four steaks. Preheat a pan (a skillet leaves a nice pattern on the meat), add the oil and cook the steaks to your liking (we recommend medium rare). Remove to a warm plate and rest for 10 minutes.

SPINACH CREAM SAUCE

20 g / 2 T butter
45 g / ⅓ C shallots, finely chopped
150 g / 5 oz fresh spinach
75 ml / ¼ C dry white wine
200 ml / ¾ C chicken stock (see p.108)
salt to taste
pepper to taste
10 g / 1 ½ t sour cream

Place the butter in a pan and heat over a moderate heat. Add the shallots and fry until golden brown. Add the spinach and stir, then deglaze with the white wine. Simmer until the liquid is reduced by half. Add the chicken stock and simmer for another four to five minutes. Blend until smooth, return to the heat and simmer until creamy. Season with salt and pepper. Reserve the sauce and sour cream for later use.

OLIVE POTATOES/POTATO PARCELS

650 g / 4 medium-sized potatoes
12 black olives, de-stoned
3 sprigs fresh Italian parsley
10 g / 1 T butter
70 g / ⅓ C mascarpone cheese
salt to taste
pepper to taste
500 ml / 2 C oil to deep fry

Peel the potatoes and cut 24 very thin slices of the same size. Top one slice with half of an olive, top the olive with a leaf of Italian parsley and cover with a second slice of potato. Press to ensure you have a tight parcel. Repeat until all slices of potato are used. Deep-fry the potato parcels in the oil until golden brown. Remove and place on a paper towel to drain. Reserve for later use.
Boil the remaining potatoes until soft, drain and mash with the butter and mascarpone cheese while still hot. Dice the remaining olives very finely and add to the mashed potatoes. Season to taste.

SUGGESTED MATCH
Sacred Hill Brokenstone Merlot

continued...

TOMATO COMPOTE

24 cherry tomatoes
100 ml / ⅓ C tomato coulis
(or whole peeled tomatoes, pureed)
salt to taste
pepper to taste
40 g / ¼ C shallots, finely diced
25 g / 2 T butter
5 sprigs fresh thyme, plucked and chopped
4 sprigs fresh thyme to garnish

Melt half the butter and sauté the shallots until light brown. Add the tomato coulis and season. Boil for three to four minutes and purée through a fine sieve. Fry the cherry tomatoes in the remaining butter for two minutes and add the chopped thyme and tomato sauce. Bring to the boil and remove from the heat immediately.

TO SERVE

Bring the spinach sauce to the boil and remove from the heat. Add the sour cream and froth with a stick blender. Pipe some of the mashed potato on the plate and stick one of the potato parcels into it. Pipe more of the mashed potato in front of the first potato parcel and repeat until three potato parcels have been used per portion. Pour some spinach sauce onto the plate and place the steak on it. Arrange the tomato compote on the plate. Garnish with a sprig of thyme and serve.

Garlic goes very well with vanilla. The sweetness of the sauce harmonises with the gamey flavour of the meat. We use canned baby pears but fresh pears can be peeled and poached in sugar water until almost soft (al dente).

NEW ZEALAND CERVENA
VENISON CUTLETS
ON VANILLA-GARLIC JUS
SERVED WITH MUSHROOM GOULASH AND SAVOURY PEAR AND PECAN NUT CAKE

CERVENA VENISON CUTLETS

4 Cervena venison cutlets (800 g / 28 oz each)

Season the cervena venison cutlets, grill to your liking (we recommend rare to medium rare) and rest them for 10 minutes.

VANILLA AND GARLIC JUS

8 cloves fresh garlic, finely sliced
30 g / 1 T honey
1 vanilla pod
500 ml / 2 C beef stock (see p. 108)
100 ml / ½ C red wine

Heat the honey in a pot and add the garlic. Leave on moderate heat until garlic is caramelised. Deglaze with the red wine. Cut the vanilla pod lengthwise in half, scrape the seeds into the red wine mixture, then add the pods. Reduce by half and add the beef stock. Simmer until the sauce reaches a syrupy consistency. Remove the vanilla pod and discard.

MUSHROOM GOULASH

150 g / ⅓ C mixed mushrooms, quartered
1 onion, sliced
10 g / 1 T paprika
5 g / ¼ C fresh thyme, chopped
75 ml / ¼ C water
salt to taste
pepper to taste

Cook the onions until light brown. Add the paprika, stir and immediately add the water. Simmer for 20 minutes. Blend with a stick blender until smooth and bring back to the boil. Season with salt and pepper. Fry the mushrooms in a little butter until soft, add just enough sauce to coat the mushrooms and cook for one minute. Adjust seasoning and add the thyme.

SAVOURY PEAR AND PECAN NUT CAKE

4 baby pears, drained
75 g / ¾ C buckwheat flour
75 g / ¾ C flour
1 egg yolk
150 ml / ½ C milk, lukewarm
5 g / 1 t yeast, fresh
30 g / 2 ½ T pecan nuts, roughly chopped
15 g / 1 ½ T butter, melted but not hot
2 egg whites, beaten until stiff
Salt to taste
4 twigs of fresh thyme to garnish

Dissolve the yeast in the milk. Add all other ingredients except the egg whites and pears and combine to form a dough. Gently fold the stiff egg whites through the mixture. Place the pears in buttered and floured medium-sized muffin tins and three-quarters fill with the dough. Bake in a preheated oven at 190°C (380°F) for 15 minutes. Leave to cool for two minutes before removing from the muffin tins.

TO SERVE

Spoon some of the jus onto the plate and place the pear cake at 12 o'clock. Put some mushroom goulash on both sides of the pear cake. Place the cooked venison cutlets on a cutting board and cut horizontally in half. Put on a slight angle in front of the pear cake. Garnish with a twig of thyme.

This fantastic curry is easy to make and really tasty. For the best possible flavour the fenugreek and the cumin should be ground just before use. The spices and the naan bread should be available in good supermarkets or Asian food warehouses.

PUMPKIN AND NUT
SPICY CURRY
WITH BASMATI RICE, MANGO CHUTNEY AND NAAN BREAD

CURRY SAUCE

6 g / 2 t turmeric
3 g / 1 t garam masala
3 g / 1 t fenugreek
6 g / 2 t cumin
2 onions, sliced
10 g / 1 ¼ t fresh ginger, finely chopped
12 g / 2 ¼ t garlic
5 g / 1 t fresh red chilli, finely chopped
40 g / 2 ¼ T tomato paste
2 tomatoes, peeled and diced
1 can (375ml) coconut cream
15 ml / 1 T oil
200 ml / 1 C water
150 ml / ½ C tomato juice
salt and pepper to taste

Heat the oil and fry all the dry spices over a moderate heat until fragrant. Add the onions, ginger and garlic and cook until onions are soft. Add the chilli and tomato paste and cook until the tomato paste loses its bright colour (approx. five minutes). Add the tomatoes, coconut cream, tomato juice and water and simmer until the sauce reaches a creamy consistency. Adjust seasoning.

PUMPKIN CURRY

400 g / 3 C pumpkin, peeled
60 g / ½ C nuts, mixed
30 ml / 2 T olive oil

Cut the pumpkin into appealing shapes for the garnish later and boil in salted water. Dice the pumpkin trimmings and pan-fry in oil. Add the nuts and curry sauce and simmer until the pumpkin is soft.

GARNISH

4 T mango chutney (see p. 112)
naan bread
fresh coriander, chopped and whole leaves
200g / 1 ½ C basmati rice, cooked

TO SERVE

Reheat the pumpkin shapes and arrange with the boiled basmati rice, mango chutney and the naan bread nicely on a plate. Garnish with the fresh coriander and serve.

SUGGESTED MATCH
Wild South Pinot Noir

A lot of work will be rewarded with a stunning vegetarian dish. To cut down on the workload, the pasta can be bought. If you cannot obtain the porcini pasta, use plain pasta and use the porcini (cèpes) in the sauce.

SPINACH
CHARLOTTE
WITH PORCINI TAGLIARINI ON
TOMATO COULIS WITH GRILLED VEGETABLE SALAD

SPINACH ROULADE

500 g / 7 C fresh spinach
20 g / 1 ¼ T butter
4 egg yolks
4 egg whites, beaten until stiff
1 pinch nutmeg
1 pinch salt
1 pinch pepper
1 clove garlic, finely chopped
350 g / 1 ½ C sun-dried tomatoes, puréed

Pan-fry the spinach with garlic and season with salt, pepper and nutmeg. Drain well in a sieve, put in a food processor with the egg yolks and purée until very smooth. Carefully fold the beaten egg whites into the spinach mixture. Spread evenly 2-3 mm (.08"-.25") thick on to an oven tray lined with buttered baking paper. Bake in a preheated oven at 180°C (360°F) until cooked (5-10 minutes).

After cooling remove the baking paper and spread the tomato purée onto the whole spinach sheet. Cut the sheet in half and roll into two skinny and tight roulades. Put the roulades for one hour in the freezer, then cut into thin slices (see photo below). Line ovenproof bowls crosswise with three strips of baking paper and butter the bowls and the paper strips. Line the bowls with the roulade slices and keep in the fridge for later use.

PORCINI TAGLIARINI

250 g / 2 ¼ C flour
2 eggs
I egg yolk
30g / ¼ C dried porcini mushrooms, finely ground
I pinch salt
15 ml / I T oil

Combine all ingredients and form a smooth dough. If the dough is too dry add some water. Rest for 30 minutes and roll to a 2 mm (⅛ ") sheet. Cut the sheets into long strips and rest until dry to touch. Cut lengthwise into fine noodles. Cook the pasta and refresh in cold water.

MUSHROOM FRICASSÉE

350 g / 4 C mushrooms, cut into small pieces
250 ml / I C vegetable stock (see p. 109)
I shallot, finely diced
salt to taste
pepper to taste
20 g / 2 T butter
4 eggs

Pan-fry shallots and mushrooms until brown. Add the vegetable jus and seasoning and simmer until reduced by half. Allow to cool. Mix the cooked tagliarini with the mushroom fricassée and gently combine with the slightly beaten eggs.

SUGGESTED MATCH
Gunn Estate Skippers Pool Sauvignon Blanc

continued...

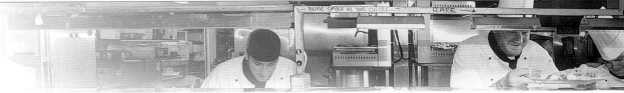

64

VEGETABLE SALAD

1 eggplant, sliced lengthwise and grilled
1 zucchini, sliced lengthwise and grilled
1 red capsicum, peeled and grilled
1 yellow capsicum, peeled and grilled
4 sun-dried tomatoes
8 black olives
60 ml / ¼ C olive oil
60 ml / ¼ C balsamic vinegar
1 pinch salt
1 pinch pepper
1 pinch sugar

200 ml / 1 C tomato coulis (see p. 111)
2 potatoes, peeled and cut into matchstick-sized sticks,
deep-fried until golden brown, for garnish

Cut all vegetables into strips and mix with the olives and tomatoes. Marinate with the rest of the ingredients.

TO SERVE

Fill the prepared bowls with the tagliarini mixture and bake in a preheated oven at 160°C (320°F) for 15-20 minutes. Turn the hot charlottes out of the bowls onto plates and cut a wedge out of each. Move the wedge slightly outwards to show the inside of the charlotte. Serve with the vegetable salad and the tomato coulis.

Thar (Himalayan mountain goat) is a highly regarded trophy animal in New Zealand, but generally under-rated as game for the table. If you cannot obtain thar it can be substituted with any other red game meat.

KUMARA
THAR BACKSTEAKS
ON RED BERRY AND MUSTARD SAUCE WITH GLAZED WITLOOF

THAR STEAKS

800 g / 28 oz thar backsteaks
50 g / ¼ C oil
salt to taste
pepper to taste

Season the meat and sear in a very hot pan. Put aside to cool. Cut the kumara into long thin strips, heat the butter in a frying pan and fry the kumara until soft and golden. Transfer into a bowl, add salt, pepper and egg whites and stir well to combine. Completely coat the prepared meat with a thin layer of the kumara mixture. Bake in a preheated oven at 230°C (450°F) for three minutes, then reduce heat to 180°C (360°F) and bake for another four minutes or until kumara coat is brown and crispy. Remove from the oven and rest for 5-10 minutes before serving.

KUMARA COAT

800 g / 3 C kumara, peeled
5 g / ½ t salt
pinch pepper
70 g / ¼ C butter
70 g / ¼ C egg whites

RED BERRY AND MUSTARD SAUCE

250 ml / 1 C beef jus (see p.108)
20 g / 1 T mild English mustard
80 g / ½ C raspberries
100 g / ¾ C strawberries
60 ml / ¼ C red wine
30 g / ¼ C shallots, diced
15 g / 1 T butter
salt to taste
pepper to taste

Sauté the shallots in butter without colouring and add the mustard. Add the red wine and reduce by half. Add the berries and jus and simmer over moderate heat until syrupy. Adjust seasoning if necessary.

GLAZED WITLOOF

4 witloof
200 ml / 1 C white wine
10 g / 1 T sugar
20 g / 1 ¼ T butter
salt to taste

Remove the stalk of the witloof to separate all leaves. Melt half of the butter and caramelise the sugar. Add the witloof leaves, stir to coat evenly with the caramel and add the wine. Simmer until all the caramel is dissolved, then add the seasoning. Slowly add the rest of the butter while stirring continuously.

GARNISH

50 g / ¼ C raspberries
50 g / 4 strawberries
4 sprigs basil

TO SERVE

Cut the thar into two slices per portion and arrange with all other items nicely on a plate. Drizzle the sauce around the plate and garnish with some fresh berries and a sprig of basil.

Hares are abundant in the Mount Cook region and a popular dish on our menu. The garnishes used complement the hare very well and create a nice harmony of flavours. Hare can be substituted with rabbit or any other game.

ROASTED
HARE SADDLE
ON WHITE BEAN AND TRUFFLE PURÉE SERVED
WITH ROASTED CELERY AND PEAR-SHALLOT JAM

HARE SADDLE

4 hare saddles
5 g / 1 ½ T thyme
5 g / 1 ½ T parsley
5 g / 1 T rosemary
40 g / ¾ C breadcrumbs
salt to taste
pepper to taste
butcher's string

Take the fillets from the inside of the saddle off the bone and trim the sinews and the fat. Starting from one side of the saddle, follow the line of the bone with a sharp pointed knife to remove the flap from the bone. Work your way around the whole saddle to remove both flaps and all the meat in one piece. Trim the silver skin off the boned saddle, reserve the trimmings and place meat-side-up on a cutting board. Place the fillets in the centre of the saddle. Combine breadcrumbs with the chopped herbs and the seasonings and sprinkle over the hare saddle. Tightly roll the saddle and tie with butcher's string. Sear the saddle in a hot pan and roast in a preheated oven at 180°C (360°F) for eight minutes. Remove from the oven and rest for 5-10 minutes.

WHITE BEAN AND TRUFFLE PURÉE

250 g / 1 ½ C white beans
10 ml / 2 t truffle oil
10 g / 1 t black truffle pieces, finely chopped
500 ml / 2 C chicken stock (see p. 108)
500 ml / 2 C cream
salt to taste
pepper to taste

Soak the beans for six hours or overnight in cold water. Strain and boil in chicken stock until soft. Add the cream and seasoning and simmer over a moderate heat for a further 30 minutes. Stir periodically to avoid burning. Remove from the heat and purée until really smooth. Adjust seasoning and pass through a sieve. Add the truffles and the truffle oil and combine well.

SAUCE

100 ml / ⅓ C red wine
300 ml / 1 ¼ C beef jus (see p. 108)

Brown the trimmings and deglaze with red wine. Reduce by half and add the jus. Simmer until the sauce is syrupy. Strain and adjust seasoning.

ROASTED CELERY

320 g / 1 ½ C celery, peeled and cut into 10-cm (4") lengths
20 g / 1 ¼ T butter
12 g / 1 T celery salt
pepper to taste

Melt the butter and add the celery. Season and sauté until golden brown. Roast at 180°C (360°F) in an oven for five minutes. Place celery on a paper towel to remove excess fat.

PEAR AND SHALLOT JAM

1 recipe (see p. 114)
4 sprigs fresh thyme for garnish

TO SERVE

Cut each cooked hare saddle into five equal slices and arrange all items nicely on a plate with the pear and shallot jam. Garnish with a sprig of thyme.

DESSERTS & CHEESES

There are many different ways to make a soufflé and generally a lot of people are afraid to try making this wonderful light dessert. The recipe we use here at the Hermitage Hotel has no flour in it and is very easy to prepare.

MOUNT COOK
SOUFFLÉ

TUILLE

1 egg white
30 g / 3 T sugar
30 g / 2 T butter
35 g / 1/3 C flour

Melt the butter in a pot, pour into a bowl and let cool until lukewarm. Combine all ingredients and mix until smooth. Rest the mixture for 20 minutes in a cool place (preferably not the fridge). While the mixture is resting prepare a template in the desired shape. We use a plastic lid with a triangular shape cut in it to imitate Aoraki - the mountain. Place the template on a greased baking tray and spread the tuille mixture thinly over it (see photos opposite). Repeat three times. Bake the tuilles in a preheated oven at 180°C (360°F) until golden brown. While the tuilles are still hot they are flexible and can be shaped into any desired shape – we bend them around a rolling pin to produce a curved shape that will fit around the ramekin the soufflé is served in (see later). Once cold remove from the rolling pin carefully and reserve for later use. Part of the tuille mixture can be coloured with cocoa, and a decorative pattern can be piped onto the tuille before baking.

SOUFFLÉ

3 eggs
60 g / 1/3 C sugar
180 g / 3/4 C sour cream
1 vanilla pod
melted butter to line 4 moulds
Sugar to dust the moulds

BERRY COULIS

1 recipe (see p. 111)

Start by preparing the moulds. Ramekins, which are fireproof porcelain dishes, are ideal. Butter and sugar the ramekins, making sure they are lined all the way up to the top, and put the prepared ramekins in the fridge. Separate the eggs, ensuring there is no trace of egg yolk in the egg whites. Put the egg whites in a very clean bowl. Mix the sour cream and the egg yolks until smooth. Cut a vanilla pod lengthwise in half and scrape out the fine seeds with the back of a knife. Add the seeds to the sour cream mixture and stir well. Add the sugar to the egg whites and whisk until stiff. Gently fold the sour cream mixture through the stiff egg whites, ensuring both mixtures are combined well. Fill the prepared ramekins with this mixture to about 5 mm (0.19") from the top. Bang the ramekins gently on a table to even out the mixture inside and put them on a baking tray for easy removal after they are baked. Bake in a preheated oven at 190°C (380°F) for 10 minutes. Do not open the oven while baking as this may collapse the soufflés. They should rise by approx. 3-4 cm (1" - 1 1/2 ") over the rim of the ramekin and have a crispy, golden brown top.

TO SERVE

Arrange fresh berries along the outside of the plate and put one tuille in the centre just where the soufflé will be. As soon as the soufflé is baked put it in its place on the plate and dust with icing sugar. Place the berry coulis in a small bowl alongside the soufflé, and serve immediately.

Tiramisu is a classical Italian dessert. Translated into English it means 'pick-me-up', a reference to the coffee in the dish. Once you make this easy but absolutely delicious dessert your guests will come back again and again for another taste.

ITALIAN
TIRAMISU
WITH PISTACHIO BISCOTTI

LADYFINGERS (SPONGE FINGERS)

2 egg yolks
15 g / 1 T sugar
2 egg whites
35 g / 3 T sugar
55 g / ½ C flour
60 g / ½ C icing sugar
125 ml / ½ C Piazza D'Oro coffee

Combine the egg yolks with the 1 T of sugar and beat until creamy. Put the egg whites in a very clean bowl and beat for three minutes, then add the 3 T sugar and beat until stiff. Fold the egg white mixture into the egg yolk mixture and gently fold in the flour. Put mixture in a piping bag with a small plain nozzle and pipe little bone-shaped biscuits on a baking tray lined with baking paper. Dust with the icing sugar and bake in a preheated oven at 200°C (390°F) until golden brown. Remove carefully from the paper while still warm. Allow to cool and reserve.

MASCARPONE CREAM

125 g / 1 C mascarpone cheese
125 g / 1 C egg yolk
35 g / ¼ C icing sugar
1 egg white
30 g / 3 T sugar
125 ml / ½ C cream
60 g / ¾ C cocoa to dust the cream

Combine the egg yolks, mascarpone cheese and icing sugar in a mixing bowl and whisk until creamy. Combine the egg whites and the sugar in a very clean bowl and beat until stiff. Whip the cream until soft peaks form. Fold the egg whites through the mascarpone mixture, add the whipped cream, and fold very gently to combine the mixtures.

BISCOTTI

1 recipe (see p. 103)

TIRAMISU

Put about 1 T of mascarpone cream in medium-sized coffee cups. Smooth and top with ladyfingers soaked in coffee. Bang the coffee cups carefully on a table to get rid of any air holes in the tiramisu. Top with more mascarpone cream. Continue the process until you have two layers of ladyfingers and a layer of mascarpone cream on top. Put in the fridge for at least three hours - overnight would be best.

TO SERVE

Before serving dust the tiramisu with cocoa and serve with the biscotti.

The Hermitage Hotel serves
and recommends Piazza D'oro Coffee.

These light quenelles make a nice finish to a menu.

You can substitute mascarpone cheese for quark, provided it is not

too runny. We use mascarpone cheese from Whitestone, a small

cheese factory in the South Island.

QUARK
QUENELLES
WITH PEAR AND LIME COMPOTE, MANUKA
HONEYCOMB AND TOASTED PUMPKIN KERNELS

SWEET BREADCRUMBS
200 g / 3 C breadcrumbs
150 g / ¾ C butter
100 g / ½ C sugar
3 g / 1 t cinnamon

Melt the butter over a moderate heat. Add all other ingredients and fry, stirring continuously until the breadcrumbs are crunchy. Cool for later use.

QUARK QUENELLES
75 g / ¼ C butter
2 egg yolks
200 g / 1 C quark
90 g / 1 C white bread
125 ml / ½ C sour cream
40 g / ¼ C semolina
75 g / ¾ C flour
2 egg whites
1 lemon, zest and juice
1 vanilla pod

Cut the crust off the bread and finely dice the bread. Combine the butter, egg yolks, lemon zest and juice, quark and vanilla seeds in a bowl and whisk until creamy. Add the bread, sour cream, flour and semolina and combine gently with the butter mixture. Whisk the egg whites until stiff and fold through the other mixture. Rest the quark mixture for an hour in the fridge. Fill a medium pot with water, add some salt and sugar and bring to the boil. With the help of a dessert spoon form quenelles and simmer for 10 minutes. Take the cooked quenelles out of the water and roll carefully in the sweet breadcrumbs.

PEAR AND LIME COMPOTE
2 pears, quartered, skin on
4 limes, segmented (see p. 116)
120 g / ½ C sugar
100 ml / ⅓ C water
15 ml / 1 t grenadine

Bring the sugar, water, grenadine and lime juice to the boil and reduce to a syrupy consistency. Add the lime segments and the pear quarters and remove immediately from the heat. Allow to cool and put in the fridge.

TO SERVE
Arrange the quenelles on a plate, spoon some of the pear compote onto the plate and place a piece of honeycomb next to the quenelles. Sprinkle the roughly chopped toasted pumpkin seeds all over the plate and garnish with the mint tip.

GARNISH
4 pieces, about 30 g / 1 oz each manuka honeycomb
toasted pumpkin kernels
4 mint tips

The frangipane tart used in our recipe is a tasty and colourful variation of a classic dish. You can either make the pastry yourself, or buy it frozen. Fresh figs can be substituted with dried figs but the high sugar content of these may make the dish too sweet.

PISTACHIO
FRANGIPANE TART
WITH FIG COMPOTE AND SEMOLINA CREAM

78

SHORT PASTRY

150 g / ½ C icing sugar
100 g / ½ C butter
150 g / 1 ½ C flour
3 g / ½ t salt
1 egg yolk

Combine all ingredients and work quickly into a dough. Avoid working for too long or it will split. Rest covered for 30 minutes before using. Roll out about 1mm (1/16 ") thick. Cut with a round pastry cutter and line four tartlet moulds 10 cm (4") in diameter. Trim the edges and leave to rest in the fridge for at least 20 minutes.

FIG COMPOTE

18 fresh figs
1 orange
1 lemon
200 g / 1 C sugar
30 ml / 2 T red wine
30 ml / 2 T lemon juice

Zest the orange and lemon, ensuring there are no white parts on the peel as they will make the compote bitter. Combine zest, wine, sugar and lemon juice in a pot and bring to the boil. Simmer until reduced by a third. Remove from the stove, add the whole figs and leave to cool. Take four figs out of the liquid and chop roughly. Place in a blender with 30 ml (2 T) of the cooking liquid and purée until smooth. Reserve.

FRANGIPANE TART

125 g / ¾ C butter
125 g / ¾ C sugar
75 g / ¾ C flour
75 g / ¾ C ground pistachio nuts
2 eggs

Place butter and sugar in a mixing bowl and beat until creamy. Add the eggs one by one while still whisking. Slowly add the ground pistachio nuts and combine gently. Add the flour and carefully mix to a smooth, creamy paste. Rest in the fridge for 20 minutes.
To make the tart, spread the puréed figs onto the prepared short pastry moulds and top with the frangipane mix. Smooth the surface and bake in the middle of a preheated oven at 180°C (360°F) for 10 minutes. Turn the heat up to 220°C (430°F) and bake for a further five minutes or until cooked.

SEMOLINA CREAM

22 g / 2 T semolina
22 g / 2 T sugar
150 ml / ½ C milk
150 ml / ½ C cream
½ vanilla pod

Combine the sugar and semolina in a bowl with a spatula and add milk, stirring to form a paste. Bring the rest of the milk, cream and vanilla seeds to the boil and stir the paste into it. Cook, stirring continuously, for two minutes, then allow to cool. Once cold, blend the set semolina cream to a thick but creamy consistency. Reserve.

TO SERVE

Spoon the semolina cream into the centre of the plate. Make an impression in the semolina with the back of a spoon and place the pistachio tart straight out of the oven on top of it. Cut the figs in half and arrange on the top of the tart. Drizzle some of the cooking liquid from the figs over the whole plate and serve immediately.

This refreshing summer dish needs ripe sweet berries

— whatever are in season, and whatever quantity you like:

the amount mentioned in the recipe is a guideline only.

Other citrus can be used instead of lemon.

SUMMER
BERRY TART
CARDAMOM PASTRY FILLED WITH LEMON CURD, TOPPED
WITH FRESH BERRIES AND SERVED WITH MACAROONS

CARDAMOM PASTRY

10 × 15 cm / 4" × 6" rolled puff pastry sheet
2 g / ¼ t ground cardamom
4 g / 1 t sugar
1 egg
20 ml / 1 ¼ T milk

Roll the puff pastry sheet on a working bench to 1 mm thick. Take a fork and punch holes in the pastry. Combine the egg with the milk and beat lightly. Brush the pastry with the egg mixture and sprinkle evenly with the cardamom and sugar. Cut circles with a 9 cm (3 ½ ") pastry cutter, then cut each circle in half. Refrigerate for 30 minutes. Bake in a preheated oven at 180°C (360°F) until golden brown. Remove from the baking tray and allow to cool.

LEMON CURD

4 lemons, zest and juice (see p. 116)
150 ml / ½ C water
35 g / ⅓ C cornflour
4 egg yolks
175 g / ⅓ C sugar

Place the lemon juice, zest, sugar and water in a pot and slowly bring to the boil. Simmer for five minutes, remove from the heat and leave to cool. Mix the cornflour and egg yolks to a smooth paste and slowly add the lemon syrup to it. Put the mixture back into a pot and stir continuously over a moderate heat until the mixture thickens and sticks to the spoon. Place in the fridge to cool.

BERRY TOPPING

1 punnet raspberries
1 punnet blueberries
1 punnet strawberries

MACAROONS

1 recipe (see p. 103)
4 mint tips for garnish

TO SERVE

Layer pastry with lemon curd nicely on a plate. Top with the washed berries — cut the berries in half if too big. Arrange the macaroons on the plate and top the tarts with berry coulis (see p. 111) if desired. Garnish with a sprig of mint.

Here are three different desserts combined as one dish.
Each has its own delicate flavour and combining them achieves a
perfect harmony. It takes some of time and effort but at the end
you have a truly memorable marriage of flavours and textures.

A DELICATE
ENSEMBLE
THREE DIFFERENT DESSERTS COMBINED AS ONE DISH

MINT PARFAIT

3 egg yolks
20 g / 1 T honey (preferably manuka)
25 g / 2 ½ T sugar
½ vanilla pod
20 g / 1 T mint liqueur
2 g / ½ t mint essence
2 egg whites
20 g / 2 T sugar
20 g / 1 ½ T chocolate, coarsely chopped
250 ml / 1 C cream
4 chocolate teardrops (see p.115)
4 mint tips for garnish

Cut the vanilla pod lengthwise in half and scrape out the fine seeds. Put the seeds, egg yolks, honey, sugar, mint liqueur and essence in a bowl. Whisk over a heated water bath (warmer than lukewarm, but not hot) until very thick and fluffy, taking care not to scramble the eggs. Take out and continue whisking until the mixture is cool again. Mix the egg whites and sugar together in a very clean bowl and whisk until stiff. Whip the cream. Now gently fold the stiff egg whites through the egg yolk mixture. Add the whipped cream and chocolate to the mixture and gently combine both mixtures. Fill the mixture into the chocolate tear drops and place in the freezer. The parfait can easily be prepared the day before – it should be given at least five to six hours in the freezer.

PASSIONFRUIT MARSHMALLOW

225 g / 1 C sugar
½ T liquid glucose
18 g / 9 gelatine sheets
1 egg white
30 g / 2 T passionfruit pulp
100 ml / ⅓ C water
icing sugar to dust
cornflour to dust
passionfruit pulp for garnish

Start by preparing a tray to set the marshmallows on. Wrap a shallow tray with cling film and dust with a mixture of equal parts of icing sugar and cornflour. Set the tray aside for later use. Soak gelatine in cold water (see p. 112). Combine sugar, water and glucose in a pot and boil to the hard ball stage, 127°C (260°F). If you do not have a sugar thermometer you can use the 'hand test': after boiling for about 10 minutes dip a spoon into the boiling sugar and then into cold water. Now try to form a ball between two fingers with the cooled sugar drop on the spoon. If this is easily done the sugar is ready; if the sugar is still too soft to form a ball continue boiling, trying continuously to form balls.

Immediately the sugar reaches the right temperature take it from the stove and add the passionfruit pulp. Stir well and add the gelatine. Mix well to dissolve the gelatine. Whisk the egg whites until stiff and slowly add the warm sugar mixture. Keep whisking until the mixture is almost cold. Quickly pour the mixture onto the prepared tray and spread evenly. Dust the surface with more cornflour/icing sugar. Put the tray in the fridge and let the marshmallows set. This will take a couple of hours. Cut the set marshmallows into desired shapes with a hot knife or round pastry cutter. Roll them in the cornflour/icing sugar mixture and set aside for later use.

MANGO TURKISH DELIGHT

1 L / 4 C water
250 ml / 1 C ginger ale
20 g / 2 T fresh ginger, grated
2 fresh mangoes
1 tinned mango
1 lemon
45 g / 24 leaves gelatine
610 g / 2 C icing sugar
10 drops rose water
icing sugar to dust
cornflour to dust
4 mint tips for garnish
4 T passionfruit pulp

Start by preparing the mango flavouring. Remove the mango flesh by cutting little segments from the pip. Boil the pip in the water and the ginger ale for 10 minutes. Cut the peel off the mango segments and discard. Cut the fresh and tinned mangoes roughly into pieces. Discard the pip, add the mango to the ginger ale mixture and boil for another 20 minutes. Blend until very smooth and strain. Put the liquid back on the stove and reduce until only 285 ml remains. Add the lemon juice and zest and the icing sugar and bring back to the boil. Strain again and add the soaked gelatine and rose water. Stir until the gelatine is completely dissolved, then add the ginger and stir well. Line a shallow tray with cling film and dust with icing sugar/cornflour mixture as used for the marshmallows. Gently pour the Turkish delight mixture into the tray. When it is almost set, again dust the top. Put the tray in the fridge until set. Cut with a hot knife into desired shapes and roll all sides in the dusting mixture. If not used immediately the Turkish delight must be stored in a very dry and cool place.

TO SERVE
Arrange the three desserts nicely on a plate and serve with passionfruit pulp.

This is a classical way of serving brie and has lots of variations all over the world. The simplicity of this dish combined with its intense flavours makes a perfect finish to a nice dinner. For best results prepare two days before serving.

TRUFFLED WHITESTONE
DOUBLE CREAM BRIE
WITH BUTTERED WHOLEMEAL BREAD

BRIE
1 round (200 g approx) double cream brie

Cut brie horizontally in half and smooth with a warm knife. Refrigerate for later use.

FILLING
60 g / ¼ C mascarpone cheese
60 g / ¼ C crème fraîche
5 g / 1 T black truffle, finely diced
3 drops truffle oil
8 g / 1 ½ T pine nuts
1 pinch salt
1 pinch white pepper

Roast the pine nuts with the truffle oil until they start to colour and set aside to cool. Using a wooden spoon gently combine mascarpone cheese with crème fraîche and carefully fold in the rest of the ingredients, including the cooled pinenuts and truffle oil. Adjust seasoning if necessary.

TO FINISH THE BRIE
Spread the filling evenly onto half of the brie and cover with the second half. If the brie was bought in a wooden box put it carefully back and close the lid without squashing the cheese. If you do not have a box, place the brie on a wooden board and cover with a cloth. The brie then needs to rest for at least six hours in the fridge.

BREAD
½ loaf wholemeal or walnut bread
200 g / 1 C butter
1 pinch salt

Cream the butter and salt until white. Cut the bread horizontally into 5mm (¼ ") slices. Spread the butter 1mm (1/16 ") thick on the slices and put them back together into loaf form. Rest in the fridge until firm.

GARNISH
10 ml / 2 t herb oil
twig of herb to match the oil
to taste cracked pepper
10 g / 2 t pine nuts, roasted

TO SERVE
Cut slices off the butterloaf, and cut those slices into finger-sized sticks. Using a hot knife cut the brie into slices without pushing the filling out of it. Arrange neatly on a plate and drizzle some herb oil around the plate. Sprinkle with the pine nuts. Garnish with the herb.

SUGGESTED MATCH
Sacred Hill Wine Thief Syrah

The best cheese to use for this lovely dish is a soft fresh goats cheese. The cheese is slightly melted onto the pear rösti and this way releases all its flavour.

MELTED
GOATS CHEESE
ON PEAR RÖSTI WITH DRIED PEAR CHUTNEY

CHEESE
80 g / 3 oz goats cheese
baby beetroot leaves for garnish

PEAR RÖSTI
2 pears, roughly grated
150 g / 4 slices white bread
2 eggs
50 ml / 3 T milk
20 g / 2 T sugar
1 pinch cinnamon
1 pinch salt
40 g / ¾ C breadcrumbs
10 drops lemon juice

Cut the bread into long sticks and combine with the other ingredients. Rest for 10 minutes. The bread should have absorbed all the added liquid. If it has not, add more breadcrumbs until there is no visible liquid and you have a dough-like consistency. Form four patties out of the mixture and pan-fry in butter until golden brown and crispy on both sides.

PEAR CHUTNEY
120 g / 4 oz dried pears, roughly diced
30 ml / 2 T cider vinegar
30 g / 3 T honey
½ chilli, small, finely chopped
1 fresh pear, cooked and finely puréed
30 g / 2 T onions, finely diced
½ cinnamon quill
1 star anise
3 g / 1 T pickling spice
1 pinch cracked pepper
30 ml / 2 T water
25 ml / 1 ½ T oil

Combine pickling spice, star anise and cinnamon with water and vinegar and bring to the boil. Simmer on moderate heat until reduced by half. Strain and cool. Sweat off the onions in oil without colouring and add the cooled vinegar reduction. Add all other ingredients and bring to the boil. Simmer until the chutney has a jam-like consistency. Adjust the seasoning if necessary and refrigerate.

TO SERVE
Place a rösti on a plate and top with the sliced goat cheese. Place under a grill until the cheese is melted. Place a small round pastry cutter onto the plate and fill it with the pear chutney. Squash down tightly and remove the pastry cutter. Garnish and serve immediately.

DINNER BUFFET

It's easy to entertain and cater for a larger group of people if you do it buffet style. Much preparation can be done two to three days in advance, which reduces the workload on the actual day. With a little planning the task of putting it all together becomes really easy and you can spend more time with your guests.

DINNER
BUFFET
FOR 12 PEOPLE

Start by making the condiments. These will keep for weeks in sterilized jars.

Flavours in the pot au feu will improve from re-heating so it is perfect for preparation well in advance.

If you tackle the task of smoking your own salmon you will get an excellent end result, but you can cut preparation time by buying cold-smoked salmon.

Salads can be made up to two days in advance. As long as you roast the lamb saddle on the day it can be prepared a day ahead. Marjoram jus can be reheated a day after preparation.

Dishes that do have to be made on the day are the curried fish, lettuce and hot vegetable and starch dishes.

1	Wild Goat Pot Au Feu
2	Green Thai Curried Gurnard
3	Roasted Lamb Saddle with Marjoram Jus
4	Mixed Bean Salad
5	Tossed Iceberg Lettuce
6	Gado-Gado Salad with Peanut Sauce
7	Home-smoked Salmon
8	Grilled Baby Octopus with Roasted Garlic
9	Basmati Rice
10	Mascarpone Baked Potatoes (p. 115)
11	Mediterranean Vegetable Ensemble (p. 115)
12	Caesar-Style Dressing (p. 110)
13	Pear and Shallot Jam (p. 114)
14	Mango Chutney (p. 112)
15	Sweet Smoked Tomato Glaze (p. 113)
16	Corn Relish (p. 113)
17	Dijon Mustard and Honey Sauce (p. 114)
18	Horseradish Mousseline (p. 114)

WILD GOAT POT AU FEU

2 kg wild goat chuck, diced
4 onions, small
3 celery sticks
12 cloves garlic
4 potatoes, large, peeled
75 g / ¾ C barley
8 juniper berries, crushed
15 g / 3 T fresh thyme, chopped
2 ½ L / 10 C chicken stock (see p. 108)
250 ml / 1 C port
80 ml / ⅓ C oil
salt to taste
pepper to taste

Cut all vegetables into large dice. Heat a large pot over moderate heat and sear all vegetables except the potatoes. Remove the vegetables from the pot. Season the goat meat and cook in the pot until evenly browned. Add the port and reduce by half. Add the chicken stock, vegetables (except the potatoes), barley, juniper berries and thyme. Cover with a lid and place in the oven at 140°C (285°F) for two hours or until meat is almost tender. Add the potatoes and put back into the oven for a further 45 minutes or until potatoes and meat are cooked. Remove from the oven, adjust seasoning and put into a serving bowl. Serve hot.

GREEN THAI CURRIED GURNARD

1.5 kg gurnard fillets
1.5 kg onion, diced
300 ml / 1 C vegetable stock
1 tin (395 ml) coconut cream
10 g green curry paste
salt to taste
pepper to taste
50 g flour
8g paprika
3g lemon pepper
5g fresh coriander, chopped
100 ml / ⅓ C oil
dill to garnish

Cook the onions until golden brown and add the vegetable stock and coconut cream. Simmer for 10 minutes over moderate heat. Add the curry paste, salt and pepper. Stir well and bring back to the boil. Remove from the heat and reserve for later use.
Combine flour, paprika, lemon pepper and coriander. Cut the fish into 50-60 g pieces and dip into the flour mixture, covering evenly. Pan-fry the fish until cooked. Arrange the fish nicely onto a platter, top with the sauce and garnish with a few sprigs of dill. Serve hot.

ROASTED LAMB SADDLE

1 lamb saddle
butcher's string
4 rabbit fillets
100 g / 6 T butter
½ bunch fresh rosemary
½ bunch fresh thyme
½ bunch fresh marjoram
salt to taste
pepper to taste
3 cloves garlic
120 g / 1 ¼ C breadcrumbs
butcher's string

Prepare the lamb saddle as for the hare saddle (see p. 68) or ask your butcher to do it for you. Reserve bones and trimmings for the sauce. Heat the butter and add the breadcrumbs, garlic and herbs. Cook until the breadcrumbs are crunchy. Season the lamb saddle and spread the bread-crumb mixture evenly over the meat. Place the rabbit fillets in the middle and roll the saddle tightly. Tie with butcher's string. Sear the meat and roast in the oven at 130°C (270°F) to a core temperature of 68°C (160°F). Rest for 10 minutes before cutting. Arrange nicely on a serving platter. Serve hot.

MARJORAM JUS

bones and trimmings from the lamb saddle
150 ml/ ½ C red wine
1 L / 4 C beef stock (see p. 108)
1 bunch fresh marjoram

Roast the bones and trimmings until brown. Add the red wine and reduce by half. Add the beef stock and simmer until the sauce is a syrupy consistency. Remove from the heat and add the marjoram. Leave to infuse for 30 minutes. Strain the sauce and adjust seasoning. Pour into a serving bowl. Serve hot.

MIXED BEAN SALAD

100 g / ½ C kidney beans
100 g / ½ C black-eyed beans
100 g / ½ C lima beans
1 red capsicum, diced
1 cucumber, diced
2 tomatoes, diced
2 onions, diced
100 ml / ⅓ C olive oil
20 ml / 1 ½ T white wine vinegar
50 ml/ 3 ½ T water
salt to taste
pepper to taste
1 sprig parsley
1 red capsicum for garnish

Soak the beans overnight in water, separately, and cook until tender. (Do not mix the different kinds, as the cooking times will vary.) Strain and combine with the rest of the ingredients. Adjust seasoning and put into a serving bowl. Garnish with red capsicums and a sprig of parsley.

TOSSED ICEBERG LETTUCE

2 heads iceberg lettuce
100 g / ¾ C beansprouts
5 red radish, grated
2 spring onions, sliced
1 carrot, grated
2 red onions, sliced
1 recipe Caesar-style dressing (see p. 110)

Shred the lettuce and mix well with all the other vegetables. Serve the salad and dressing in separate bowls.

GADO-GADO SALAD

150 g / 1 C packed Chinese cabbage
150 g / 1 C green beans, boiled, 3-cm pieces
150 g / 1 C cucumber, cut into 3-cm sticks
150 g / 1 C carrot, cooked, 3-cm sticks
5 eggs, hardboiled, cut into segments
1 head lettuce, shredded
150 g / 1 C beansprouts, blanched
3 potatoes, peeled, boiled & diced
300 g / 2 C bean curd (tofu), diced and deep fried

PEANUT SAUCE

300 g / 3 C peanuts, roasted and ground
2 cloves garlic, crushed
1 t Indonesian shrimp paste (blanchan)
3 red chillies, deseeded
20 g / 1 T tamarind pulp
125 ml / ½ C water
2 T brown sugar
40 g / ¼ C shallots, finely chopped
3 lime leaves
10 g / 1 t ginger
650 ml / 2 ½ C coconut cream
4 T olive oil
salt to taste

GARNISH

prawn or shrimp crackers
fried shallots

Put tamarind in a cup, top with boiling water and mix. Rest for one hour and strain. Discard the tamarind and reserve the juice for later use. Blend the chillies and shrimp paste in a food processor until smooth. Heat the olive oil in a frying pan over moderate heat and cook the paste until the flavours are released. Add the shallots and garlic and cook for a further three minutes. Add the peanuts, lime leaves and ginger and stir well. Add the tamarind juice, salt and brown sugar, stir to combine and add the coconut cream. Bring to the boil and remove from the heat.

TO SERVE

Put the peanut sauce in a bowl and place it into the middle of a big platter. Arrange all vegetables nicely around the sauce. Garnish with the crackers and fried shallots.

HOME-SMOKED SALMON

2 salmon fillets (approx. 1.8 kg/ 4 lb)
150 g / ½ C rock salt
75 g / ⅓ C sugar
20 g / ⅓ C packed fresh dill, chopped
pepper to taste

Mix salt, sugar, dill and pepper. Sprinkle evenly on both sides of the salmon fillets. Marinate for 24 hours. Wash the fillets thoroughly and pat dry.
Put for 12 hours in the cold smoker; use sawdust of your liking (we use manuka/New Zealand tea-tree.) Cut the salmon into very thin slices and arrange neatly on a platter.
If you do not have a cold smoker, use this simple but effective method. Put some sawdust in the bottom of a baking dish. Put a grille into the dish and place the salmon on it. Cover the dish tightly with foil. Place the dish over high heat on the stove and as soon as the sawdust starts to smoke stand the dish in cold water. Leave for 20 minutes. Repeat this process four to five times or until the salmon develops a nice smokey flavour.

GRILLED BABY OCTOPUS WITH ROASTED GARLIC

1.5 kg / 11 C baby octopus
1 carrot, grated
1 courgette, grated
12 cloves garlic, thinly sliced
15 g / 1 t brown sugar
1 sprig fresh rosemary
30 ml / 2 T olive oil
30 ml / 2 T white wine vinegar
30 ml / 2 T mirin
salt to taste
pepper to taste
5 star anise
1 cinnamon stick

Pan-fry the octopus until cooked and transfer into a bowl. Heat the olive oil over moderate heat and add the garlic and brown sugar. Cook until golden brown, add the rosemary and mix with the octopus. Combine mirin, vinegar, salt, pepper, star anise and cinnamon and bring to the boil. Remove from the heat and rest for 30 minutes to infuse flavours. Strain and add the vinegar mixture and the grated vegetables to the octopus. Carefully mix the salad to combine all ingredients. Fill into a serving bowl and decorate with rosemary.

BASMATI RICE

8 portions basmati rice, cooked

Put the boiled rice into a serving bowl and decorate with some chopped parsley. Serve hot.

100

Provided you garnish the rum torte on the day, it can be prepared the previous day, and macaroons and biscotti keep for up to a week in an airtight container. The toffee crumble can be put together a day before you bake it.

1   Rum Cream Torte

2   Banana Toffee Crumble

3   Chocolate Layered Mint Parfait

4   Macaroons

5   Biscotti

6   Chocolate Sauce (see p. 110)

7   Berry Coulis (see p. 110)

RUM CREAM TORTE

Sponge fingers (Ladyfingers) 4 times the recipe (See p. 72)

Place a 28cm (11") cake ring on a base. Combine coffee and rum and soak the sponge fingers in it. Line the bottom and the side of the cake ring with the soaked sponge fingers. Reserve for later use.

CRÈME

100ml / ½ C milk
40 g / 3 T sugar
10 g / 5 gelatine leaves
1 egg yolk
½ vanilla pod
1 pinch salt
20 ml / 2 T rum
1 egg white
500 ml / 2 C cream
250 ml / 1 C Piazza D'Oro coffee
20 ml / 1 T rum
20 g / ¼ C sliced almonds

Soak the gelatine in cold water until soft. Remove from the water and squeeze out any excess liquid. Put the egg white into a very clean bowl and whisk with half the sugar until stiff. Whip half of the cream. Scrape the seeds from the vanilla pod and put into a metal or glass bowl. Add the milk, rest of the sugar, egg yolk, gelatine and salt. Beat this mixture over steam until it is very light and creamy and starting to thicken. Take off the steam and continue whisking until the mixture is cool. Slowly add the rum, whisking continuously. Gently fold the stiff egg whites through the yolk mixture and carefully add half of the whipped cream. Stir slowly with a wooden spoon to combine.

Put a third of the crème into the prepared cake ring and top with more soaked sponge fingers. Cover these with another third of the crème, followed by another layer of soaked sponge fingers. Now add the rest of the crème and finish with a top layer of soaked sponge fingers. Put into the fridge to set for at least six hours.

Take the torte out of the cake tin and whip the other half of the cream. Spread two-thirds of it evenly onto the torte and cover the sides with the almonds. Pipe rosettes around the edges of the torte with the remaining cream and sprinkle with the almonds. Put a sponge finger on each rosette. Cut the torte into portions and put it on a serving platter.

BANANA TOFFEE CRUMBLE

1 tin (395 ml) sweetened condensed milk
125 g / ½ C sugar
250 g / 1 ½ C butter
375 g / 3 C flour
10 bananas

Place the unopened tin of condensed milk in a pot of water and boil for three hours, topping the water up if necessary. Remove tin and allow to cool. Combine flour, butter and sugar in a bowl and rub between your fingers until crumbly. Cover and rest in the fridge for one hour. Peel and roughly chop the bananas and combine with the condensed milk, which should be golden brown. Put into a fireproof bowl and top with the crumble mixture. Bake in a preheated oven at 180°C (360°F) for 30 minutes or until the crumble mixture is golden brown. Remove from oven and place hot on the buffet.

CHOCOLATE LAYERED MINT PARFAIT

mint parfait (see p. 82) 3 times the recipe
200 g / 7 oz chocolate

When you make the parfait, leave the chocolate out of the recipe. Fill a loaf tin or bowl 10 mm deep with the parfait mixture and put in the freezer for 20 minutes. Melt the chocolate and spread a very thin layer onto the mint mixture. Add another layer of mint mixture, another layer of chocolate and put back in the freezer for 20 minutes. Repeat until all the mint mixture is used up, ensuring you finish with a layer of mint mixture. Leave in the freezer for five hours or until frozen. Take out of the tin and cut into slices. Arrange on a platter and garnish with mint leaves.

MACAROONS

90 g / 1 C fine desiccated coconut
180 g / ¾ C sugar
3 egg whites

Combine all ingredients in a pot and cook over low heat, stirring continuously until the mixture reaches 60°C / 140°F (about five minutes). The mixture should not colour while cooking. Allow to cool. Put mixture into a piping bag with a small star nozzle and pipe small amounts on a lightly greased baking tray. Bake in a preheated oven at 180°C (360°F) until golden brown.

BISCOTTI

225 g / 1 ⅓ C plain white flour
200 g / 1 C sugar
2 g / 1 t salt
3 g / 1 t baking powder
2 eggs, beaten
½ pod vanilla
zest and juice from half a small orange
zest and juice from half a small lemon
100 g / 1 C roasted almonds, finely chopped
30 g / ¼ C pistachios, roughly chopped

Follow this sequence strictly: first sift together all the dry ingredients except the nuts. Then add the nuts and combine. Lightly beat the eggs in a mixing bowl and add to the dry ingredients. Add the orange and lemon juice and zest and then the seeds of the vanilla pod. Mix well to combine and form a log 4 cm (1 ½ ") diameter. Bake in a preheated oven at 190°C (380°F) for 15 to 20 minutes or until golden brown. Allow to cool and cut the log into slices ½ cm (¼ ") thick. Arrange the slices on a baking tray and put them back in the hot oven for 10 to 15 minutes to dry.

HERMITAGE
WINE MATCHES

THE FOLLOWING DISHES HAVE BEEN MATCHED WITH
A WINE PROUDLY SUPPLIED BY SACRED HILL

Spicy Tortilla Soup - page 10
GUNN ESTATE SILISTRIA SYRAH

Greenshell Mussels - page 30
SACRED HILL WHITE CABERNET

Pumpkin and Apple Soup - page 12
WILD SOUTH CHARDONNAY

Baby Salmon - page 38
SACRED HILL RIFLEMANS CHARDONNAY

Seared Lamb Fillets - page 16
SACRED HILL WINE THIEF MERLOT

Lamb Rack Roulade - page 48
SACRED HILL BP MERLOT CABERNET

Smoked Salmon Mille-Feuille - page 20
SACRED HILL SAUVAGE
SAUVIGNON BLANC

Marinated Beef Fillet - page 54
SACRED HILL BROKENSTONE MERLOT

Tuna Medallions - page 22
SACRED HILL BARREL FERMENTED
CHARDONNAY

Pumpkin & Nut Spicy Curry - page 60
WILD SOUTH PINOT NOIR

Five Spice Duck Leg - page 24
SACRED HILL MARLBOROUGH
PINOT NOIR

Spinach Charlotte - page 62
GUNN ESTATE SKIPPERS POOL
SAUVIGNON BLANC

Trio of Scallops - page 26
SACRED HILL MARLBOROUGH
RIESLING

Double Cream Brie - page 86
SACRED HILL WINE THIEF SYRAH

STOCKS, SAUCES & CON

DIMENTS

Following is a compilaton of various stocks and sauces commonly used throughout the recipes in this book. Using ice-cold water in stocks will make the finished product clear and helps intensify the flavours.

BASIC
STOCKS & SAUCES
USED THROUGH-OUT THE RECIPES IN THIS BOOK

BEEF STOCK OR JUS
Makes 1 L
250 g beef bones, small pieces
750 ml / 3 C red wine
10 g / 2 t tomato paste
2 L / 8 C water, ice-cold
salt to taste
1 onion
1 carrots
2 sticks celery
1 bay leaf
1 clove

Place the bones in a roasting pan and roast at 200°C (390°F) until evenly brown, turning occasionally. Dice the vegetables, add to the bones and continue browning. Drain and discard the fat from the pan, and add the tomato paste. Continue roasting for another five minutes and add a third of the red wine. Reduce until the liquid is gone and repeat twice more. Transfer to a large pot and add water. Add the salt and bring to the boil. Reduce the heat, skim off the scum and add the bay leaf and the clove. Simmer for five to six hours and strain.

CHICKEN STOCK
Makes 1 L
500 g chicken bones
1.2 L / 5 C water, ice-cold
salt to taste
1 onion
1 carrot
1 small leek
2 sticks celery
2 sticks bay leaf
1 clove

Wash the bones in cold water and place in a large pot. Add the water and salt and bring to the boil. Reduce the heat and skim off the scum. Add the rest of the ingredients, simmer for two hours and strain.

FISH STOCK

Makes 1 L

500 g fish bones
1.2 L / 5 C water, ice-cold
salt to taste
50 ml / ¼ C white wine
25 g / 1 1 ⅓ T butter
1 onion
1 small leek
2 sticks celery
1 bay leaf
1 clove

Dice the vegetables small and sauté in butter. Add the washed and roughly cut fish bones and continue to sauté for a further three minutes. Add the white wine, water, salt and bring to the boil. Reduce the heat and skim off the scum. Add the rest of the ingredients. Simmer for 30-40 minutes and strain.

VEGETABLE STOCK

Makes 1 L

25 g / 1 T butter
1.2 L / 5 C water
salt to taste
1 carrot
1 onion
1 small leek
2 sticks celery
1 bay leaf
1 clove

Sauté small diced vegetables in butter. Add ice-cold water, salt and bring to the boil. Reduce the heat and skim off the scum. Add the rest of the ingredients. Simmer for 30-40 minutes and strain.

VEGETABLE GRAVY

Makes 1 L
500 ml / 2 C red wine
30 g / 2 T tomato paste
2 L / 8 C water, ice-cold
salt to taste
2 onion
2 carrots
4 sticks celery
1 small leek
2 cloves garlic
1 bay leaf
1 clove

Cut the vegetables into medium dice and roast at 200°C (390°F) until evenly brown, stirring occasionally. Add the tomato paste and continue roasting for another five minutes. Add a third of the red wine. Reduce until the liquid is gone and repeat twice more. Transfer to a large pot, add the water and salt and bring to the boil. Reduce the heat, skim off the scum and add the bay leaf and the clove. Simmer for one hour and strain.

CAESAR-STYLE DRESSING

Makes 1 L
90 g / ⅓ C anchovies
2 eggs
pepper to taste
salt to taste
16 g / 1 T mild English mustard
1 t Tabasco sauce
4 cloves garlic
30 ml / 2 T lemon juice
60 g / 1 C parmesan cheese, grated
30 ml / 2 T Worcestershire sauce
30 ml / 2 T soy sauce
170 ml / ⅔ C balsamic vinegar
540 ml / 2 C olive oil

Combine all ingredients except the oil and whisk until it starts to thicken. While still mixing add the oil slowly. Adjust seasoning if necessary.

TOMATO COULIS

Makes 1.5 L

10g / ½ T butter
½ carrot
½ onion, peeled
2 garlic cloves, roughly chopped
2kg / 4 lb tomatoes, quartered
20g / 2 ½ t tomato paste
2 bay leaves
10 black pepper corns
2 sprigs fresh basil
250ml / 1 C tomato juice
500ml / 2 C water
salt to taste
pepper to taste

Heat the butter in a medium-sized pot and fry the roughly chopped onions until translucent. Add the roughly chopped carrots and fry for a further two minutes. Add the garlic, stir well and add the tomato paste. Fry for three or four minutes and add all other ingredients. Bring to the boil, reduce the heat and simmer for 20-30 minutes. Purée the sauce through a sieve or mouli, bring back to the boil and adjust seasoning.

BERRY COULIS

Makes ½ L

400 g / 3 C mixed berries
150 g / ¾ C sugar
(more or less depending on sweetness of berries)
60 ml / ¼ C water

Bring the water and berries to the boil and add the sugar. Simmer for two minutes, adjust the sweetness and pass through a fine sieve. Leave to cool, cover and put in the fridge till needed. This can be stored for three to four days.

CHOCOLATE SAUCE

Makes ⅓ L

150 ml / ½ C water
60 g / ⅓ C sugar
30g / ⅓ C cocoa
100 g / 1 C chocolate

Bring the water to the boil and add the rest of the ingredients. Simmer until the chocolate is dissolved and strain through a fine sieve.

The following is a compilation of various condiments commonly used with the recipes in this book. Be sure to read the tips on p. 116 to perfect your condiment dishes.

VARIOUS
CONDIMENTS
USED WITH THE RECIPES IN THIS BOOK

VEGETABLE SALSA

20 g / ⅛ C red onions, finely diced
30 g / ¼ C yellow capsicum
1 tomato, deseeded and diced
30 g / ¼ C zucchini, finely diced
30 g / ¼ C fennel bulb, finely diced
30 g / ¼ C eggplant, finely diced
15 ml/ 1 T sunflower oil
1 clove garlic, crushed
20 g / ⅛ C pine nuts, roasted
15 g / 2 T capers
5 g / 2 T basil, finely chopped
5 g / 2 T Italian parsley, finely chopped
1 g / 1 t chives, chopped
10 g / 1 ½ T sultanas
20 ml / 1 ½ T white wine vinegar
40 ml / 3 T extra virgin olive oil

Cut the capsicum into quarters and place skin-side-up under a grill. Leave until skin gets black, then put the capsicum in a sealed plastic bag and allow to cool. Peel the capsicum and finely dice. Sauté fennel, zucchini, garlic and eggplant for two minutes and season well. Leave to cool and mix with all other ingredients. Rest in the fridge for one hour.

MANGO CHUTNEY

1 mango, roughly diced
50 g / ⅓ C onion, diced
80 g / ¼ C tomato, peeled and chopped
100 g / 2/3 C apple, peeled, cored & chopped
15 g / 2 T raisins
15 g / ⅛ C ginger, minced
5 g / 1 t garlic, crushed
salt to taste
30 g / 1/6 C brown sugar
75 ml / ¼ C malt vinegar
20 ml / 1 T lemon juice
100 ml / ⅓ C water

Combine all ingredients and marinate for 12 hours. Simmer over moderate heat, uncovered, until the mixture reaches a thick consistency – about two hours. Allow to cool. Do not use any aluminium equipment for this recipe as it oxidises. The chutney can be kept in preserving jars for up to three months.

SWEET SMOKED TOMATO GLAZE

600 g / 5 large acid-free tomatoes
25 g / 2 T butter
70 g / ½ C onions
3 cloves garlic
2 g / ½ t chilli flakes
50 ml / 3 ½ T cider vinegar
50 ml / 3 T red wine vinegar
50 g / 3 T brown sugar
35 g / 2 T molasses
3 g / 1 t pickling spice
35 g / 2 T tomato paste
5 ml / 1 t Worcestershire sauce
15 g / 1 T cornstarch
65 ml / ¼ C soya sauce
pepper to taste

Combine tomatoes, garlic and onions in a shallow dish and put for ½ hour in the hot smoker. Mix with all other ingredients except the cornstarch and simmer over moderate heat for two hours. Pass through a sieve or mouli and bring to the boil again. Dissolve the cornstarch in a little water and stir into the boiling sauce. Boil for three to four minutes to a syrupy consistency and cool.

CORN RELISH

200 g / ¾ C corn kernels
30 g / ¼ C red capsicum, finely diced
30 g / ¼ C green capsicum, finely diced
68 g / ½ C red onions, finely diced
3 g / ½ t garlic, crushed
1 pinch turmeric
10 g / 2 t sugar
60 ml / ¼ C water
20 ml / 1 ½ t white wine vinegar
2 g / 1 T fresh coriander, chopped
4 g / 1 t cornstarch
salt to taste
pepper to taste
20 g / 2 T butter

Combine water, vinegar, sugar and turmeric in a pot and bring to the boil. Add the corn kernels and cook until tender. Dissolve the cornstarch in a little water, stir into the sauce and boil for a further five minutes. Remove from the heat and cool until lukewarm. Add the rest of the ingredients and leave in the fridge for a day to combine and infuse all flavours.

PEAR AND SHALLOT JAM

160 g / 1 C pears, peeled and diced
80 g / ½ C shallots, sliced
1 g / 1 t loose fresh thyme, chopped
30 g / 2 T sugar
80 ml / ⅓ C red wine
30 ml / 2 T red wine vinegar
1 g / ½ t arrowroot
2 g / ½ t grenadine
20 g / 1 ½ T butter
1.5 g / 1 leaf gelatine leaves
30 ml / 2 T water

Melt the butter over moderate heat, add the pears, shallots and thyme and cook without colouring until soft. Add the sugar, wine, grenadine and vinegar and reduce by two-thirds. Dissolve the arrowroot in a little water and add to the mixture. Boil for five minutes and remove from the heat. Soak the gelatine in cold water, strain and add to the pear mixture. Stir well to combine and allow to cool and set.

DIJON MUSTARD AND HONEY SAUCE

40 g / 3 T Dijon mustard
20 g / 1 T honey, melted
10 ml / 2 t yoghurt
20 ml / 4 t vinegar
1 T fresh dill, plucked and chopped

Combine all ingredients and adjust seasoning.

HORSERADISH MOUSSELINE

200 ml / 1 C cream, whipped
25 g / 1 T fresh horseradish, grated
6 drops lemon juice
salt to taste
pepper to taste

Carefully combine all ingredients and adjust seasoning.

MASCARPONE BAKED POTATOES

10 potatoes, large
100 g / 1 C mascarpone cheese
pepper to taste
salt to taste
chives to garnish

Wash the potatoes, put on an oven tray and bake until soft at 190°C (370°F). Cut the potatoes in half and scoop out the flesh. Reserve the skins. Combine the potato, mascarpone cheese, salt and pepper and stir well to combine. Fill the potato skins with the mixture and put back into the oven until hot. Arrange potatoes nicely on a platter and garnish with some chives

MEDITERRANEAN VEGETABLE ENSEMBLE

8 onions, sliced
4 red capsicums, sliced
2-3 eggplant, round slices
4 courgette, oval slices
12 tomato, round slices
4 sprigs fresh thyme, chopped
150 ml / ½ C extra virgin olive oil
6 cloves garlic, crushed
50 ml / 1 T sunflower oil
salt to taste
pepper to taste

Cook the onions in the oil until golden brown and add the capsicums, salt and pepper. Continue cooking until the capsicums are cooked with a little bite left. Line a fireproof bowl with this mixture and sprinkle with the thyme. Mix the olive oil with the garlic. Lay one slice of eggplant onto the mixture and continue, alternating the vegetables, to lay slice by slice very tightly, like scales. Brush the vegetable layer with some of the olive oil mixture and season. Bake in a preheated oven at 120°C (250°F) for 1 ½ hours, brushing periodically with the oil mixture.

CHOCOLATE TEARDROPS

90 g / 1 C dark chocolate, roughly cut
6 flexible plastic strips
21 cm (8") long
4.5 cm (1 ¾ ") wide

Put the chocolate in a stainless steel bowl and place in a hot water bath. Melt the chocolate while stirring. Do not heat to over 37°C (body temperature). Cut six flexible plastic strips 21cm (8") long and 4.5cm (1 ¾ ") wide, and spread the melted chocolate 1mm (1/16 ") thick onto the plastic strips. Fold the ends of the plastic strips together and fasten with a paper clip (see dessert at top, p.85). Put in fridge to set the chocolate.

TIPS

TIPS

PEELING TOMATOES

Core the tomatoes at the stem end and score a cross at the opposite end. Put them into boiling water for 30 seconds then drop them into a bowl of ice water. Peel off the skin with a small pointed knife.

SOAKING AND DISSOLVING GELATINE

Put the gelatine, leaf by leaf, into a bowl of cold water and leave to soak until soft. Remove from the water and squeeze out any excess liquid.
To dissolve, add to hot ingredients or put in a metal bowl, place on the stove and melt while continuously stirring. Never boil gelatine, as it will not set properly.

SEGMENTING CITRUS FRUITS

Top and tail the citrus fruit and place on a cutting board. Cut the peel off the flesh, ensuring you get no white skin. Holding the peeled fruit over a bowl, cut along the white skin to free the segments. This catches the juice that inevitably falls when segmenting.

ZESTING A CITRUS FRUIT

Zest is the outer peel of citrus fruits. To zest a citrus fruit either use a zester, or peel the fruit carefully with a sharp knife, ensuring you get none of the white inner pith, then slice the peel very thinly. If zest is required as well as juice or segments in a recipe, always do the zesting first.

HERMITAGE CUISINE
INDEX